Multinational investment in developing countries

Multinational investment in developing countries

A study of taxation and nationalization

Thomas Andersson

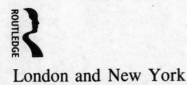

London and New York

First published 1991 by Routledge
11 New Fetter Lane, London EC4P 4EE

Simultaneously published in the USA and Canada
by Routledge
a division of Routledge, Chapman and Hall, Inc.
29 West 35th Street, New York, NY 10001

© 1991 Thomas Andersson

Phototypeset in 10pt Times by
Mews Photosetting, Beckenham, Kent
Printed in Great Britain by
Biddles Ltd, Guildford and King's Lynn

British Library Cataloguing in Publication Data
Andersson, Thomas, *1959–*
    Multinational investment in developing countries : a study
    of taxation and nationalization.
    1. Developing countries : foreign investment.
    Multinational companies
    I. Title
    332.67314

    ISBN 0–415–06219–5

Library of Congress Cataloging-in-Publication Data
Andersson, Thomas.
        Multinational investment in developing countries : a study of
    taxation and nationalization / Thomas Andersson.
            p. cm.
    Includes bibliographical references and index.
    ISBN 0–415–06219–5
        1. Investments, Foreign–Developing countries. 2. International
    business enterprises–Taxation–Developing countries. I. Title.
    HG5993.A57 1991
    336.24'3–dc20
                                                            90–27021
                                                                CIP

To my parents

Contents

Part III Nationalization of multinational enterprise affiliates

Figures

Tables

Acknowledgements

I have had many sources of inspiration for this work. During my research, I found that the subject attracted considerable interest in scattered corners of the world. In spite of a voluminous literature in the field, observers in diverse locations and positions shared a view, perhaps for different reasons, that some crucial links and relationships had so far been bypassed. My ambition was to build on the knowledge and insights accumulated in economics while trying to explore some new avenues of approach.

The task would not have been possible had it not been for many colleagues and friends. Lars Bergman, Claes-Fredrik Claeson and Mats Lundahl, Stockholm School of Economics, and Henrik Horn, the Institute for International Economic Studies, Stockholm, provided good advice and encouraging support during my work. I am also grateful to Magnus Blomström, Stockholm School of Economics, for valuable suggestions for improvements while going through my final draft. Furthermore, my opponent James Markusen, Western Ontario, provided most constructive and insightful comments.

A special mention must be made of Kurt Brännäs, University of Umeå, to whom I am much indebted for invaluable co-operation in joint work partly overlapping this study. Special thanks are also due to Dale Jorgennson, Harvard University, who kindly supported me during one year's study at the Economics Department, and provided important clues to solutions of some of the problems encountered.

Moreover, it is gratefully acknowledged that the fundamental ideas in this work were first articulated in exciting discussions with Richard Caves, Jeffrey Sachs and Raymond Vernon, Harvard University. For valuable comments and suggestions for improvements concerning game theory I thank Jörgen Weibull at the Institute of International Economic Studies, Stockholm, Paul Segerström, Michigan State University, and Stefan Lundgren, the Industrial Institute for Economic and Social Research, Stockholm.

For comments on various drafts, I am also grateful to Jan Bojö, Claes Magnus Cassel, Peter Hagström, Ari Kokko and Pär Ronnås, Stockholm School of Economics, Susan Collins, Kala Krishna, Kevin O'Rurke, Joakim Stymne and Peter Timmer, Harvard University, Mark Gersovitz, Princeton University, Padma Malampally, UNCTC Bangkok and New York, Lars Ljungkvist, University of Wisconsin, Claes Timrén, Svenska Handelsbanken, Lennart Flood, Gothenburg University, and Johan Åshuvud, the representative of IUCN in Central America, who tragically died in a car accident in 1988.

Thanks are due to Mario Zejan and Renato Aguilar, Gothenburg University, for assistance with computer programming, Stephen Kobrin, Wharton School of Business, and Michael Minor, University of Tulsa, kindly provided their data bases on forced divestments. Annaclara Gonzalez drew my figures with great patience. Rune Castenäs is thanked for his truly trustworthy support in financial and practical matters.

My research has been financed by Jakob Wallenberg's Fund and Svenska Bankforskningsinstitutet. The Fulbright Commission, Stockholm School of Economics, and The Swedish Institute financed my time at Harvard University. Furthermore, a grant from the Royal Swedish Academy is acknowledged.

Words of thanks are also due to my family and many good friends who supported me throughout. Many are worthy of mention. Finally, this work is devoted to my parents, Inez and Bertil, who gently bestowed me with curiosity and concern about the world. Although my father did not live to see the final version of this work, he is my deepest source of inspiration.

Needless to say, any remaining mistakes or omissions are entirely mine.

Thomas Andersson

Part I
Introduction

1 Statement of the issues

INTRODUCTION

A considerable proportion of the flows of goods and factors between countries takes place within multinational enterprises (MNEs).[1] As an operative definition we associate this with firms which own and control income generating assets in more than one country (cf. Buckley and Casson 1985). A subsidiary owned and controlled abroad is established through direct investment. According to conventional theory, discussed in Chapter 2, direct investment is motivated by specific advantages associated with ownership, combined with advantages in internalization and inter-country differences in factor costs and technology (Dunning 1977).

A more profound understanding of MNEs is certainly needed, but can in any case explain only half the impact of (foreign) direct investment on resource allocation and social welfare. This depends on the behaviour of firms, as well as that of countries. Although political motives certainly matter for countries' behaviour, there is considerable evidence that economic factors are of great importance. With sovereign nation states, there are no universal or reliable rules for the division of profits across national boundaries.

Beginning in the 1970s, there has been a general change of course in economics. It has become clear that, in an imperfectly competitive world, the actions of one agent affect others, and that this interaction is taken into account by everybody when acting. Traditional 'structural' approaches have now become supplemented by 'strategic' ones, which allow agents to adapt to changes in each others' behaviour. The analytical tools have gradually been refined. New insights into the role of expectations, the nature of equilibria, sequential bargaining and time consistency have revised our view of, for example, monetary and fiscal policy, public finance and inter-country policy co-ordination (see, for example, Selten 1975; Lucas 1976; Kydland and Prescott 1977; Rubinstein 1982; Binmore and Herrero 1984; Shaked and Sutton 1984; Barro and Gordon 1986).

There has been a similar revision of the view of international capital flows. Following Eaton and Gersovitz (1981), imperfections in the standard model of international borrowing have been examined in a number of studies (Sachs and Cohen 1982; McFadden *et al*. 1985; Hajivassiliou 1987; Bulow and Rogoff 1989a). Much of this literature is concerned with interaction between sovereign debtor nations and perfectly competitive creditors. Concerning direct investment, Hartman (1985) and Newlon (1987), among others, have investigated home country behaviour in the form of tax treatment of foreign source income. Hines (1987) has taken into consideration the response of host country governments to US tax increases. Most opportunities for strategic behaviour prevail in the interaction between countries and large firms, however, especially as improved information and administrative capacity enhance the ability of governments to discriminate policies between firms. The most palpable influence is likely to be exerted by host countries whose gains to some extent directly offset the profits of MNEs.

Clarifying the consequences of strategic interaction between MNEs and host countries should be an important research agenda for the 'new course' in economics. This is particularly important for the developing countries, which are host to some 25 per cent of the world's direct investment but home to only about 3 per cent. Owing to this asymmetry, they benefit primarily as hosts, and must be expected to do the best they can in this capacity. These countries also have a particularly great need of the capital, technology and human skills that direct investment can provide.

For a long time, MNEs were believed to require protection from their home governments in order to prevent host countries from expropriating gains earned under their jurisdiction. Much of the world's history in the last two centuries has, in fact, been shaped by the desire of the leading industrialized countries to safeguard the undertaking of profitable business operations abroad. This has led to many clashes with less developed capital-importing countries. The attitudes towards foreign firms became hostile, particularly in the 1960s, and Gilpin (1975) predicted difficult times for investors with declining US hegemony in the world economy. Today, however, this hostility seems to have mostly disappeared, and the general atmosphere in developing countries leans more towards harmony and co-operation.

The MNE – host country relationship was from the beginning viewed as a bilateral monopoly, with the two sides struggling over the structuring of projects and the division of gains. Penrose (1959) argued that a foreign firm should receive as much profit as induces it to invest. Kindleberger (1965) considered that this was only a lower limit, and added an upper limit set by the scarcity value to the host country of the services provided by an investment project. Most subsequent work in the field builds on the studies by Vernon (1971) and Moran (1974) who added the time dimension and the role of risk. Their findings are referred to as the theory of 'obsolescing bargain' or the 'changing balance of power'. The idea is that, over time, there is a shift in the bargaining position to the advantage of poor countries as they attain a higher level of development and investment projects become sunk.

Among the empirical studies of host country behaviour *vis-à-vis* direct investment, those preceding 1980 mostly lacked comprehensive data. In the last decade, nationalization has been studied by, for example, Jodice (1980), Kobrin (1980, 1984) and Minor (1987, 1988). Other policies have been examined by, for example, the Harvard Multinational Enterprise Project, directed by Vernon,[2] and Guisinger (1985). Most of this work has provided useful information on cross-country variation in policies at a certain time, but developments over time have not been satisfactorily examined. Among the formal models allowing for strategic interaction, Eaton and Gersovitz (1983, 1984) determined time-consistent equilibria with regard to taxation and nationalization respectively. Shenfeld (1984) investigated host country policies pursued by an individual country, and Doyle and van Wijnbergen (1984) analysed taxation when there is competition between host countries. However, these studies have not resolved some of the pertinent issues left unanswered by the empirical studies. The theoretical work on nationalization has generally not explained its occurrence, and studies of taxation have tended to assume perfect competition and zero profits, thereby neglecting the distribution of gains from direct investment.

To gain as much as possible from direct investment, host countries may use a variety of policies, ranging from those that aim at a general and sweeping transformation of the domestic economy, to measures that target MNEs directly. There is no general formula to establish which are the most effective. For the transfer of technology to developing host countries, Blomström and Wang (1989) indicate that support of domestic firms may be preferable to imposition of performance requirements on the behaviour of MNEs. However, throughout the developing world, there has for decades been an abundance of policies which interfere with MNEs directly. This study is concerned with such policies.

Although there are many diverse host country policies *vis-à-vis* MNEs, we can think in terms of two broad categories. On the one hand, there are policies which stimulate certain kinds of behaviour on the part of MNEs. Among them are, for example, regulations, tax incentives and subsidies. On the other hand, there are policies which interfere with the ownership and control of MNEs, such as joint ventures, licensing agreements and, in the extreme, complete takeover by the host country. The former are referred to here as *taxation*, the latter as *nationalization*.

Currently, there is general uncertainty regarding the extent to which the nature of MNE–host country conflict impedes or distorts the potential welfare effects of direct investment. The threat of adverse host country behaviour for example, has been put forward as a partial cause of the decline in direct investment that has occurred in developing countries in the 1980s. Liberalization of the foreign investment regime, with a reduction of burdens and restrictions, is a standard part of the policy package advised by the International Monetary Fund to countries afflicted by balance of payment difficulties. Moreover, a multilateral insurance agency was instituted in association with the World Bank in the mid-1980s to encourage equity investment by alleviating investors' concerns about non-commercial risks. At first, it caused controversy, and had to await ratification from the required number of countries. The host country attitudes have gradually become more favourable, however, and the Multilateral Investment Guarantee Agency (MIGA) was established in April 1988.[3]

In this book we investigate the impact of host country behaviour on the undertaking of direct investment and the distribution of gains. Most of the questions addressed have already been dealt with in a voluminous literature. However, we add to most previous work by considering that direct investment is traded in a market where it is supplied by firms and demanded by countries. In this market, we consider competition between host countries, real profits and alternative host country policies. On the basis of theoretical models which allow for strategic interaction and pay attention to co-ordination problems, we come up with new explanations of host country policies and results which partly contradict mainstream views. Some hypotheses are formulated and tested against empirical data.

In this chapter we introduce the issues to be studied. The first section reviews the history of direct investment and 'foreign property rights' is surveyed in the next section. Particular attention is paid to the extension of these rights to developing countries and their subsequent gradual breakdown. In the following section, we are concerned with host country policies from the late 1960s, and point out the importance of economic motives for nationalization and taxation of MNE affiliates in this period. Next we survey the flow of direct investment in the last decades, comparing the trend with those of direct investment in other parts of the world, as well as other capital flows to developing countries. Finally, we summarize the chapter and present an outline of the book as a whole. Owing to the extent of the ground covered, the presentation is sweeping and only major circumstances and events are discussed.

THE HISTORY OF FOREIGN PROPERTY RIGHTS

Property rights should be expected to be crucial for the undertaking of direct investment, the purpose of which is control through ownership in another country. The meaning of property cannot be taken for granted, however, but is rooted in the social and institutional heritage of a society, which is subject to continuous change. It is even more difficult to justify any *a priori* or moral vision of property across the boundary of jurisdictions. Nevertheless, or perhaps because of this state of facts, there have been repeated violations of 'foreign property rights' for more than a hundred years.

Itinerant merchants in the Middle Ages were protected only by local municipal laws. Foreign property rights evolved as orderly national economies developed in Europe, and commercial treaties were set up between them bilaterally. By the mid-nineteenth century, foreign property rights had been well defined in Europe and gradually became codified as international law. According to the basic principles, foreigners were subject to local law. Additional minimum standards deemed interference with foreign property permissible only in exceptional cases, then requiring 'prompt, adequate and effective' compensation.

Foreign property rights emerged initially as a result of reciprocal interests. They facilitated capital flows and international economic specialization between nations. Within Europe, they were supported less by the threat of coercion than by the withdrawal of normal reciprocities. The extension of rules beyond Europe was different, as can be exemplified by the 1838 Anglo-Turkish Convention. Essentially, this meant that a 300-year-old tradition of mutual commercial privileges was replaced by a treaty which forced the Ottoman Empire to open its markets for European goods. The same course was followed in the Anglo-Chinese wars of 1839–42 and 1856–60, the Anglo-Japanese treaties of 1854 and 1858, consular arrangements in Africa and similar arrangements by the other major European powers with countries outside Europe. Throughout, this resulted in both a modern structure of property rights and commercial penetration.

Outside Europe, foreign property rights served to establish and maintain order in a system of diverse and unequal countries. Their extension reflected the increasing military strength of the capital exporting countries: '. . . international property rights were effectively guaranteed by the extraterritorial application of European and American laws', (Lipson 1985: 14). Concerning the policies of Great Britain, Platt (1968: 353) states that the call was not for special privilege, but 'equal favour and open competition for British finance and trade overseas'. This is shown by the reliance on most–favoured–nation treaties. In Africa and Asia, however, outright colonialism was accompanied by an over-representation of direct investment from the colonial powers, especially the smaller ones (Svedberg 1981).[4] In Latin America, Great Britain rejected territorial ambitions after the defeats in the Rio de la Plata region in 1806–7.

Until the 1890s, bonds were the major kind of investment in Latin America, with Great Britain owning three-quarters of the region's foreign debt. Latin America welcomed foreign investment, but disputed the rights of investors to call on outside powers for assistance at times of dispute. There were, indeed, many defaults as well as disputes. The British government was unwilling to defend individual subjects, but determined to steer off general assaults on property rights. Generally it did not have to, because British denial of further credit was a powerful tool, particularly after the Franco-Prussian War crippled its major competitors and London attained a near credit monopoly. This ensured the settlement of most defaults.

The British stock of direct investment grew rapidly from the early 1860s and surpassed the outstanding value of bonds by the 1890s. This was not surprising since the rate of return was considerably higher. Most of this investment was concentrated in railways and public utilities. Britain turned out to be more ready to intervene by force to defend direct investment than in the case of default. On the whole, there were at least forty examples of British military intervention in Latin America between 1820 and 1914, and a great many were primarily concerned with the protection of direct investment.

Soon after its independence, the United States emerged as a champion of property rights. This ambition became more predominant as the country's economic and political expansion began in the late nineteenth century. At the time of the First World War, the United States became the greatest investor in Latin America, mainly through direct investment in agriculture, mining and oil. Like Britain, the United States firstly signalled an unwillingness to intervene in private activities. However, the Roosevelt Corollary of 1903 declared a duty and responsibility to intervene in the American continents on behalf of all foreign investors. European entanglement was prevented, but the United States became compelled to retaliate wherever foreign property rights were threatened. The result was a stream of coastal landings, armed interventions, involvement in civil wars etc.

Despite growing military intervention in the early twentieth century, there were as yet no real disputes over the nature of foreign property rights. Expropriation for example, was universally viewed as robbery, and conflicts tended to concern countries' right to enforce rules bilaterally. The Hague Conferences at the turn of the century produced fragile compromises on this issue. Thus, the nature of foreign property rights remained intact until the Soviet nationalizations in 1918, which represented the first real challenge. The United States failed to raise support for military retaliation or to organize a unified set of economic sanctions. The Soviet Union exploited the individual interests of the Western powers and concluded agreements bilaterally, step by step reopening its market for foreign investment. Unofficially, however, and contrary to the British strategy, the United States blocked settlements that would have acknowledged the right to nationalize.

The Soviet nationalizations demonstrated the weakness of international law. In the following decades, the poorer countries became more active in the League of Nations, where all countries had the same voting power, and the poor soon outnumbered the industrialized countries. The diplomatic process began to dilute the traditional norms. Sovereignty was increasingly stressed, and partial rather than full compensation from nationalization advocated. However, the United States and some other capital exporters continued to defend traditional property rights with great determination. Unlike the Soviet Union, poor countries had little opportunity to resist either military or economic retaliation. Turkey, Mexico and Bolivia nevertheless undertook nationalizations that departed from traditional rules, and got away with them. With a world war on the horizon, the United States had to make choices between the protection of investment and the need for stable allies. Military intervention could result in chaos, causing higher costs than revenues, which meant that the very weakness of expropriating countries could be to their advantage.

After the Second World War, the United States sought to reconstruct an open world economy. One step was a charter for world trade, along with which the United States brought up investment security, arguing for the traditional principles of prompt, adequate and effective compensation. As discussed by Lipson (1985), this measure was self-defeating. In 1952, a resolution by the General Assembly of the United Nations endorsed nationalization of natural resources. In 1962, compensation standards were diluted as 'appropriate' compensation was called for in Resolution 1803 on Permanent Sovereignty over Natural Resources. In

1972, the conditions justifying nationalization were stated to be irrelevant. Finally, in 1974, the Charter of Economic Rights and Duties of States placed the rights with host countries, and the duties with firms and capital-exporting countries.[5]

Despite the disputes, most direct investment remained secure until the late 1960s. Passing resolutions is not the same as passing international law, and the defence of traditional rights continued. One aspect of the US resistance to relinquishing its investment protection was the country's long-lasting refusal to sign the UN Convention on the Recognition and Enforcement of Foreign Arbitral Awards, which was signed by twenty-five countries and came into force in June 1959. Among other things, the Convention precluded the courts of the states that signed from interfering in conflicts covered by an arbitration clause. The benefits of predictable and uniform arbitration rules were downplayed relative to the desire to make extraterritorial applications of the US securities laws. Even after pressure from private organizations finally made the Senate consent to accession to the UN Convention in 1970, US courts have continued to protect US investors abroad by preserving their litigation rights (cf Ishizumi 1984).

An important victory for investment security was achieved at Bretton Woods with the creation of the World Bank and the International Monetary Fund. In contrast with the United Nations, voting power was based here on capital contributions, placing power in the hands of the capital-exporting nations. The World Bank was mandated to encourage direct investment, and protected foreign investment by denying credit to expropriating countries. According to a 1971 memorandum, the Bank does not lend or appraise projects in countries that expropriate foreign equity.

In particular, the United States, Britain and France continued to respond bilaterally. However, the legitimacy of intervention in order to protect foreign property rights had been gradually undermined by the diplomatic process. The need to take account of this change, and the subsequent investment disputes in Cuba, Brazil, Honduras, Ceylon, Argentina etc., moved the leading home countries towards a stern and mandatory system of economic retaliation. In the United States, the Hickenlooper Amendment (1962) and the Gonzales Amendment (1972) made suspension of aid legally mandatory *vis-à-vis* countries that 'fail to provide adequate compensation' when nationalizing, or in other ways violating, foreign property rights. In addition to economic retaliation, military action was taken overtly or covertly. Chile constituted a conspicuous example of the latter in 1973.

Despite the continued defence, there was a marked increase in nationalization of direct investment in the late 1960s and early 1970s. Moreover, the policy was now pursued by a majority of developing countries, acting independently of their political ideology. This development was set off by a range of factors – the continued struggle for sovereignty, the political gains of regimes in newly independent former colonies to acquire domestic control over their natural resources *and* a diminishing capacity for the industrialized countries to strike back as an increasing number of developing countries nationalized more or less simultaneously.

Although the United States in particular went on retaliating against countries that violated the traditional norms on 'too massive' a scale, or 'too conspicuously', it turned out that, in effect, there was no mandatory and indiscriminate defence of foreign property rights. For instance, the United States accepted actions in Venezuela and Saudi Arabia which in 1951 in Iran had led to a complete boycott by Britain and the United States, the overthrow of Mossadegh and the installation of the Shah. The traditional norms had broken down in the sense that not only was legitimation gone, but there was no longer any effective enforcement.

Why did no consistent defence of foreign direct investment develop, despite bilateral and multilateral attempts? Although the complete answer may be complex, it would appear that such a policy was no longer in the interest of the capital-exporting countries, or even the MNEs themselves. Referring to the subsequent period, Lipson (1985) wrote 'the automatic application of sanctions would only sever their future profits. . . . self-reliance and accommodation is more prudent – and more profitable' (Lipson 1985: 226).[6] Continued inflexible resistance from home countries would have had less chance than previously of being effective and could have led to renewed violation. Open conflict dramatized the role of direct investment, and provoked host countries to strike with nationalistic fervour against the 'representatives of colonialism'. Continued tension between home and host countries would have held up the political gains obtained by regimes in the Third World from treating MNEs as scapegoats in times of domestic crisis.

Summing up it can be concluded that foreign property rights grew out of reciprocal interests, but that they were one-sidedly extended to the developing countries. The capital exporters laid down the 'rules of the game'; the capital importers sought to undermine them. At first, the latter sought to establish the right not to be subject to military intervention at the time of investment disputes. Subsequently, they struggled for the right to nationalize foreign-controlled firms, for whatever gains. By diplomatic co-operation, the developing countries gradually undercut the traditional foreign property rights. Some home countries still continued to defend these rights despite increasing lack of legitimacy. In the late 1960s, however, a majority of the developing countries nationalized direct investment without any mandatory and consistent response from the capital-exporting countries.

MULTINATIONAL ENTERPRISE–HOST COUNTRY RELATIONS FROM THE LATE 1960s

The violation of the traditional rights discussed in the preceding section – nationalization or expropriation – was characterized by Truitt (1974) as the point on a continuum where government action has the effect of depriving foreign investors of wealth. Over time, the concept has gradually become more diluted and diffuse. Here, it is used in the sense of 'forced divestment of ownership', as defined by Kobrin (1980) (see further Chapters 2 and 5). Because the definition of foreign direct investment entails managerial control exercised through equity ownership across national borders, nationalization is thought of as leading to the involuntary withdrawal of the targeted MNE, with or without compensation from the host country.

Further in line with Kobrin (1984), we distinguish between 'mass' and 'selective' nationalizations. The former generally target firms indiscriminately throughout industries and encompass most or all foreign property – and sometimes all private property.[7] They have normally occurred in systems that have exploded after periods of tension, following a systematic national change such as decolonization or Marxist revolutions. Although there have been exceptions, most mass nationalizations have been part of a general transformation from a market to a socialist economy. In contrast, selective nationalizations tend to target a limited number of firms.

There is no doubt that mass nationalizations generally have a strong political or ideological content. Selective nationalizations, in contrast, seem to be driven primarily by economic motives. While we shall return to their characteristics later, it can be noted here that selective nationalizations are systematically related to firm- and industry-specific factors which reflect economic costs and benefits. Although the distinction between mass and selective nationalization, and even more between political and economic motives, is difficult or impossible to make in all cases, it is still believed to be valid in a broad sense.

As discussed in the preceding section, the period up to the late 1960s was marked by a regime of fierce responses from the leading capital exporters when foreign property rights were violated. Substantial costs had to be expected by countries which challenged the traditional norms. Most nationalizations, or about 60 per cent of all acts, during that period belonged to the mass category. The MNE–host country relationship then entered a new phase. The number of nationalizations rose, as did the number of countries that nationalized, acting independently of their political and ideological orientation. While mass nationalizations continued to result in fierce responses from the major home countries, the increase in the total number of acts from 1968 was accounted for by selective nationalizations, which now made up some 80 per cent of the total. Kobrin (1984) concluded that, for the whole period 1960–79, only ten out of a total of seventy-nine nationalizing countries belonged to the mass category.

Consequently, the real change from the previous period was the emergence of selective nationalizations, which could be pursued without dramatic and expensive conflicts with home countries. There were no longer any clear rules, or enforcement of rules. The subsequent stage has been described in words such as 'we are entering an era of great uncertainty. The world economy will undoubtedly be characterized by a confused and complex mixture' (Gilpin 1975: 261).

Thus, the spurt in nationalization was not due to any increase in ideological conflict. Nor was it caused by the developing countries acting as puppets or dummies. In contrast with the mass nationalizations of the past, the selective nationalizations were primarily generated by economic motives. In the late 1960s Third World governments had become more stable and sophisticated. They were now more capable than previously of using nationalization as a measure to make economic gains. The policy was generally inconspicuous and often accompanied by incentives to obtain new investment. An ambiguity in host country behaviour had become evident – on the one hand the desire to expropriate, and on the other the need to attract new investment.

The host country policies pursued from this time have sometimes been referred to as 'creeping nationalization'. Some of the policy instruments aim at manipulating the behaviour of MNEs rather than depriving the parent companies of ownership. The dividing line is far from clear cut in practice. Limitations to ownership and control such as requirements of joint ventures may, for example, be combined with various incentives and restrictions to achieve the outcome desired by the host country. Nevertheless, the two categories of taxation and nationalization are fundamentally different in nature. The former hinges on a host country's capacity to share the gains of a foreign run activity, and the latter on its capacity to run that activity on its own (see further Chapter 2).

Bergsten *et al.* (1978) and Leonard (1980), among others, argued that during the 1970s the developing countries attained administrative, managerial and technical capabilities that enhanced their capacity to extract gains from direct investment through taxation. The data available are scanty, particularly on effectiveness, but there was certainly a proliferation of controls and performance requirements aimed at balance of payments operations, transfers of technology etc. Thus, parallel to the increasing intensity of nationalization in the early 1970s, there was also an increase in taxation.

The general trends did not encompass all developing countries. Concerning taxation, there were relatively few regulations and restrictions in most of Africa and Asia, although there were numerous incentives for the purpose of attracting direct investment. In Africa, many states enacted 'investment codes' which promoted both domestic and foreign investment. Most Asian countries adopted measures which specifically facilitated direct investment. Few sectors were closed to direct investment and it was often accepted that disputes were settled through international settlements. The Arab countries had relatively less liberal systems that contained more regulations and restrictions. The generally most restrictive approach was pursued by the Latin American countries. Two regulatory models can be distinguished (Correa *et al.* 1984). Mexico and most of the Andean countries used relatively more compulsory regulation. The other Latin American countries, including Central America, developed a more incentive-oriented approach (see further Hood and Young 1979; UNCTC 1988).

At the international level, attempts were made to develop a system that would restrict the behaviour of MNEs in line with national priorities. Since the MNE is a global organization which can escape the policies of individual nations, it was argued that its behaviour should be controlled internationally. The idea, first brought forward by Goldberg and Kindleberger in 1969, of an institution corresponding to the General Agreement on Tariffs and Trade (GATT) for the international corporation was not realized despite the work of several conferences. The development of a Code of Conduct attained more palpable results. The aim was to develop a set of guidelines with which MNEs would have to comply. A draft was set up in 1982 by an inter-governmental working group although no consensus has yet been achieved. International work on the behaviour of MNEs has also been carried out within the Organization of Economic Co-operation and Development (OECD), the UN Commission on International Trade Law (UNCITRAL), the International Labour Organization (ILO) etc.[8]

At the national level, the trend towards more adverse host country behaviour shifted in the second half of the 1970s. Nationalization reached its peak in 1975 with a total of eighty-three acts in 1 year. The number of acts thereafter declined markedly, to reach practically zero in the 1980s. Concerning taxation, some controls and requirements increased throughout the 1970s, and continued to do so in the 1980s. In the wake of the 'debt crisis' of many developing countries, the Centre on Trans-national Corporations (UNCTC 1988) speaks of a growing use of performance requirements relating to exports and pressures for local content. Without doubt, there have been mounting requirements for shared ownership in joint ventures. As will be seen in Chapter 7, however, there was a marginal or non-existent increase in host country tax earnings, a general decline in performance requirements and an increase in investment incentives for US MNEs between 1977 and 1982. In addition, labour relations have been controlled, infrastructure has been provided, restrictions concerning profit repatriation have been diminished, special export-processing zones offering particularly generous conditions have been developed etc. This general trend has most recently been clearly demonstrated by Contractor (1990). Thus, the developing countries have turned from conflict towards liberalization and harmonization with MNEs in terms of nationalization as well as taxation.

To sum up, there was an increase in nationalization and taxation from the late 1960s up to the late 1970s. This development seemed to be a continuation of an old trend, although the conflict was now between MNEs and host countries and less than previously between countries. The spurt in nationalization was accounted for mainly by selective acts, which aimed at economic rather than political gains for the host country. The policy was mostly inconspicuous and accompanied by endeavours to attract new investment. In the late 1970s, the general trend was reversed. Nationalization diminished after having reached a peak in 1975, and most kinds of taxation also became more favourable to investors. The state of confrontation seemed to be over.

THE FLOW OF DIRECT INVESTMENT

In the 1960s, the total flow of direct investment grew faster than gross national product (GNP) in the world's market economies, and as fast as world trade. In the 1970s, there was a 15 per cent increase per annum in current dollar terms, which meant a rate of growth equal to that of GNP but lower than that of trade. In nominal terms, the flow of direct investment more than doubled between 1975 and 1985, but the record high was reached in 1981. From this level, it fell by more than 13 per cent to 1985. Figure 1.1 illustrates direct investment world-wide, in the developed market economies and in the developing economies from 1970 to 1984.

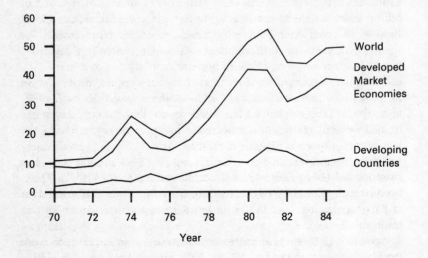

Figure 1.1 Foreign direct investment inflows by major regions, 1970–85, in billions of dollars (the socialist economies are excluded)
Source: UNCTC 1988

It should be noted that the United States provided about half of all direct investment in the early 1970s. In 1985, the US share had declined to a quarter, and Western Europe had become the major source with about 50 per cent. Japan's share had also jumped from about 5 per cent in the early 1970s to 11 per cent in 1985. Meanwhile, the United States started to capture a significant share of the inflows from 1978, attracting MNEs particularly from Western Europe and Japan.

As can be seen from Figure 1.1, the developing countries have obtained a relatively small share of the total flow of direct investment. In the downturn of the early 1980s, they fared relatively worse than the developed countries. In the late 1970s, the developing countries hosted 28 per cent of the total stock of direct investment. In the mid-1980s, they had only about 23 per cent. Meanwhile, direct investment declined relative to other capital flows in the developing countries. While the real value of direct investment hardly increased at all from 1967 to 1982, there was a yearly 9.5 per cent increase in real long-term private lending. Furthermore, reinvested earnings constituted a growing share of direct investment. In the 1980s, it accounted for about 50 per cent.[9]

All in all, the flow of direct investment has diminished in relative importance in the developing countries. There was a certain revival in 1986, however, with the total rising from an estimated average of $10 billion a year in 1983–5 to $12.5 billion. As for the future, the World Bank (1987) and UNCTC (1988) forecast a continued increase. The former prophesied that direct investment in the developing countries would average some $17 billion a year up to 1995.

The regional distribution in the developing world in the 1970s is shown in Table 1.1. Latin America attracted the bulk of direct investment, although South and East Asia became an increasingly important destination. The flow to Africa stagnated until the late 1970s, when there was a certain revival. The flow to West Asia fluctuated considerably including substantial negative figures, while developing countries in Europe attracted a negligible amount. Meanwhile, direct investment has been concentrated in a fairly small number of developing countries. This is particularly true of the 1980s. In 1980–5, eighteen countries and territories attracted 86 per cent of the flow of direct investment to developing countries. Those that continued to attract direct investment were mainly rich in natural resources, and had large markets or highly skilled and inexpensive labour forces. Africa and Latin America obtained relatively less direct investment than they did in earlier periods. Asia, particularly the southeastern part, obtained relatively more.

In terms of sectors, direct investment in information intensive services such as banking, finance, insurance etc. has become more important world-wide in the last decade, although this investment has mostly been concentrated in industrialized countries.[10] Concerning other sectors, it has been argued that the decline in investment in natural resources in developing countries was due to the fall in commodity prices from the mid-1970s. In manufacturing and some other sectors, the fall in investment followed a decline in profitability in the early 1980s. This is generally believed to be associated with heavy external indebtedness and low growth rates, particularly in Latin America and Africa. There is considerable uncertainty regarding the role of host country policies.

SUMMARY AND OUTLINE OF THE BOOK

As we have seen, foreign property rights were initially extended to the developing countries by capital exporters, but the former sought to undermine these rights through international diplomatic co-operation. While the industrialized countries fought for investment security,

Table 1.1 Inflows of foreign direct investment by regions of developing countries, 1970–80 (in millions of dollars)

Regions of developing countries	1970	1971	1972	1973	1974	1975	1976	1977	1978	1979	1980
Latin America	815.0	1,555.6	1,019.5	2,389.0	1,894.2	3,428.8	1,749.1	3,082.3	4,059.0	5,396.7	5,249.1
Africa	369.0	852.5	570.0	603.2	689.1	302.3	431.8	678.3	565.9	2,028.4	2,197.9
West Asia	142.0	−133.4	192.2	−468.5	−3,557.4	2,288.7	−1,086.4	1,056.6	855.1	−980.6	−3,097.6
South and East Asia	486.0	561.7	780.6	1,425.8	1,445.6	1,709.6	1,690.2	1,437.2	1,888.0	2,286.8	3,230.4
Europe	22.0	27.1	22.8	28.6	39.7	35.2	46.2	59.5	78.9	87.9	84.6
Total	1,834.0	2,863.5	2,585.1	3,978.1	508.7	7,764.5	2,830.9	6,313.9	7,446.9	8,819.2	7,654.3

Source: UNCTC 1983

developing countries fought for sovereignty, which initially meant the right not to be subject to intervention. Subsequently, sovereignty was interpreted as the right to nationalize for whatever gains.

There was no smooth erosion of foreign property rights. Different actors came in to defend them at different times: home country governments, syndicates of creditors, multilateral organizations etc. There was a visible relationship between the use of retaliatory action and the costs associated with social disorder or the loss of allies. When the legitimacy of these rights no longer prevailed, the home countries still continued to defend them. In the late 1960s, however, a majority of the developing countries nationalized direct investment without consistent retaliation by the capital-exporting countries.

Through their stern defence of investments up to the late 1960s, the major home countries suppressed the potential conflict between MNEs and host countries. Up to this point, most acts of nationalization were of a 'mass' character, where all foreign investors were treated more or less on the same basis. During this period, political motives largely predominated. The increase in the number of nationalizations at that time was accounted for by 'selective' acts, governed primarily by economic motives and undertaken independently of the ideological orientation of the host countries.

Parallel to the increasing intensity of nationalization, there was also an increase in taxation of MNE affiliates as the developing countries became more capable of extracting gains from direct investment under foreign ownership. Because of these developments, the MNE–host country relationship became highly infected in the first half of the 1970s. In the late 1970s, however, nationalizations became less frequent, and were practically at a standstill in the 1980s. Taxation policy was also generally on the retreat, and the broad trend in the MNE–host country relationship switched from conflict towards harmonization and liberalization.

The flow of direct investment to developing countries declined in importance in the 1970s and 1980s, relative to both direct investment world-wide and other capital flows to developing countries. The flow also became more concentrated to a fairly small number of developing countries favourably endowed with investment opportunities. For the next decade, an investment revival has been forecast in the developing countries.

This exposition leaves some pertinent questions unanswered. After the breakdown of mandatory and reliable rules in the international arena, there have been different policy regimes in different countries, but fairly universal trends in the taxation and nationalization policies across countries. The fundamental mechanisms behind the policy changes are still unclear. This paves the way for a partly new analytical approach. Building on theoretical models that allow for strategic interaction within a market for direct investment, this study aims at providing some answers to questions such as the following: When and to what extent do host countries pursue taxation or nationalization? Under what circumstances is direct investment prevented or distorted by host country behaviour? Is there a *raison d'être* for interference in the market for direct investment? The theoretical findings are applied to direct investment in pollution intensive activities and empirical investigations of the nationalization policy. The latter include analyses of the pattern of nationalization between 1968 and 1979, and the reasons for the cessation of nationalization in the late 1970s.

Of course, the developments in the real world have been influenced by changes in political and social attitudes. This study is concerned only with economic aspects of the MNE–host country relationship. Moreover, there are limitations to the economic analysis. As already indicated, this study is confined to direct investment, which means that alternative forms of MNE activity are excluded and host country policies are considered only in 'pure' forms. In addition, no attempt is made to provide a general equilibrium theory or jointly determine different host country policies. The latter may be defended by the fact that different policies are likely to be the most effective with respect to different kinds of direct investment. Finally, the empirical tests allow only for a tentative verification of the analytical framework developed.

The study is organized in four parts. The first, which includes the present chapter and Chapter 2, introduces the issues to be studied, The second, Chapters 3 and 4, is concerned with variants of the taxation policy. The third, Chapters 5–7, deals with nationalization. Conclusions and policy implications are presented in the fourth part, in Chapter 8. The chapters are outlined below.

Chapter 2 presents the theoretical background of the MNE–host country relationship. The nature of MNEs and their potential impact on host economies are surveyed. This is followed by a discussion of the basic motivation of MNEs and host countries. The behavioural options open to the respective parties are presented together with their possible consequences. It is argued that important developments in host country behaviour in the last decades cannot be explained by the theory of the 'obsolescing bargain'. Finally, the foundation of the present work is laid out.

Chapter 3 uses a game-theoretical approach to analyse the taxation of MNE affiliates when there is competition between host countries.

The set-up is the most applicable to export-oriented investment and nationalization is ruled out. Time inconsistency in host country behaviour, which is known to prevent direct investment in the one firm–one country case, is shown normally not to prevail when there is effective competition between host countries. The distribution of gains turns out to depend on the dissimilarity between countries and the 'mobility' of investment projects. The investment incentive determined by Doyle and van Wijnbergen (1984) is found to emerge as a special case.

By investigating host country competition for direct investment which causes negative external effects on the environment, Chapter 4 shows to what extent the findings of Chapter 3 continue to apply when there are external economies. Effective host country competition is seen neither to cause a level of environmental protection which is socially too low nor to distort the pattern of investment. While the findings are consistent with some observations of the real world, there are deviations due to imperfections in the international capital market and in information, for example, and 'governmental failure'.

Chapter 5 deals with nationalization of MNE affiliates. It is shown that selective nationalizations, interpreted here as targeting investment projects on a random basis, can be compatible with continued undertaking of direct investment. In the case of two countries which compete for gains from direct investment, it is demonstrated that co-ordination problems may give rise to two alternative equilibria. In one, both countries nationalize, while in the other, neither of them does. Hypotheses are derived for the factors that may cause shifts from one state to the other. Implications for welfare effects and the possible *raison d'être* for interference with host country behaviour are discussed.

Chapter 6 reviews empirical work which has sought to explain cross-country variation in nationalization. Based on the preceding chapter, hypotheses are formulated in order to explain variation in the occurrence and frequency of the policy in the period 1968–79. Because these years constitute the period in which nationalization peaked around the developing world, it is argued that countries' need and ability to earn foreign exchange, rather than the risk of discouraging direct investment, determined which countries nationalized. The hypotheses set up are largely supported by a probit and a binominal model test. The conclusions suggest a reinterpretation of previous work in the field.

Chapter 7 analyses the termination of nationalization among the developing countries in the late 1970s. A statistical test for the duration of nationalization supports the hypotheses that the termination was caused by access to inexpensive borrowing, a fall in commodity prices and the increasing indirect effect of the discouragement to direct investment for an individual country which continued when most others had terminated. Together with the results of Chapter 6, these findings tentatively support the notion of multiple equilibria in host country behaviour. Moreover, it is discussed whether the threat of nationalization still plays a role today, and whether this calls for intervention by the international community.

Finally, Chapter 8 concludes the study and discusses the implications of our findings for further studies and for policy-making.

2 Theoretical background

INTRODUCTION

Over the years there have been systematic and swift policy shifts among host countries in the developing world towards foreign investment. As seen in the previous chapter there was, for example, a rapid increase in nationalization in the late 1960s and early 1970s, and an even more abrupt termination of this policy in the late 1970s. The universal nature of these shifts suggests that the behaviour of the developing countries is interdependent in some sense.

To understand the shifts that have occurred in host country policies from the end of the 1960s, we cannot limit ourselves to considering the legitimation and enforcement of foreign property rights. On the contrary, countries should be viewed as sovereign agents that act as best they can in order to gain from direct investment. Hence, they must then take account of how the investing MNEs respond to their policies. In this chapter we survey the theoretical aspects of the the MNE–host country interaction, and we introduce a partly new framework for the purpose of analysing the fundamental determinants of host country policies in the absence of reliable foreign property rights.

The chapter is organized as follows. The next section presents the nature of direct investment, and discusses how it can affect the welfare of a developing host country. The following section is concerned with the basic motivation of MNEs and host countries, and provides a simple illustration of what is open for bargaining. The options of the respective actors are introduced next, and then possible effects of host country policies are discussed. We then argue that the policy shifts that have occurred in the last decade cannot be understood in terms of a 'changing balance of power'. A partly new framework of analysis is outlined in the penultimate section, and the chapter is summarized in the final section.

THE NATURE OF DIRECT INVESTMENT

Traditional international economics did not provide a satisfactory explanation for the existence of MNEs. Inter-country differences in the rate of return to capital can explain portfolio investment, but not direct investment. The traditional theory of the firm was similarly insufficient for the extremely imperfect markets in which direct investment occurs. Over the years, a number of theories have addressed the phenomenon. One classification is in 'macro-oriented' approaches, based on international trade, versus 'micro-oriented', based on industrial organization. The former include the currency premium theory (Aliber 1970), the dynamic comparative advantage theory (Kojima 1973), and possibly the level of development theory (Dunning 1981). The latter include the product-cycle theory (Vernon 1966), the risk-diversification theory (Grubel 1968), internalization theory or the transactional approach (Kindleberger 1969; Caves 1971; Buckley and Casson 1976) and the eclectic approach (Dunning 1977).

The division between macro- and micro-oriented theories is somewhat illusory. Part of the difference depends on which aspect of direct investment is examined. The macro-oriented theories do not explicitly consider how firms behave. Since host country action requires an understanding of how MNEs behave, it is the 'micro-economic' theories which are of interest for our purpose. These are generally based on Hymer (1960), who noted that firms suffer a handicap in foreign markets relative to domestic ones. Direct investment requires costs that are sunk, and an MNE must possess firm-specific advantages to be competitive abroad. This ruled out perfect competition as incompatible with direct investment. Kindleberger (1969) and Caves (1971) narrowed the gap to neoclassical economics by pinning down factors which may give rise to MNEs: imperfections in goods markets and factor markets, economies of scale and government-imposed disruptions. Building on Coase (1937) and Williamson (1975), Buckley and Casson (1976) explained the control of foreign firms by imperfections in information regarding, for example, technology, product quality or skills.

The earlier work was synthesized by Dunning (1977) in the 'eclectic' theory or OLI framework, according to which the undertaking of direct investment requires three cornerstones: ownership advantages, locational advantages and internalization of activities within a firm.[1] Meanwhile, three broad kinds of direct investment can be identified: First, horizontal multiplant enterprises with production abroad of essentially the same line of goods; Second, vertically integrated subsidiaries which serve the purpose of enabling transfers of intermediate products; Third, diversified affiliates which are neither horizontally nor vertically related to the rest of the organization. As discussed by Caves (1982), the determinants of the three kinds are somewhat different, but they fit into the OLI framework.

Building on Lall and Streeten (1977), we can identify some sources of oligopolistic advantages, advantages of direct investment over trade and advantages of direct investment over licensing. These are merely enumerated in the following.

1 Sources of oligopolistic advantages:
- Cheaper capital owing to the financial strength of the parent company. However this is unlikely to induce direct as opposed to portfolio investment.
- Capitalization on the exchange risk and the relative hardness of the home country's currency. This was pointed out by Aliber (1970) as the predominant motive for direct investment. Valued against empirical evidence, it is today regarded as an insufficient explanation for direct investment.
- Superior management compared with local firms.
- Superior technology and/or ability to make efficient use of it.
- Superiority in marketing – same as above.
- Superior access to raw materials owing to control over final markets, transportation, processing or the production of a material itself.
- An advantage in facilities which enjoy economies of scale owing to the availability of finance and expertise to set up and operate them.
- A superior ability to extract concessions and investment incentives from the host country government, i.e. an advantage in terms of bargaining and political power.

2 Sources of advantages of direct investment over trade:
- Cost of production in the host country relative to the home country or third countries.
- Government policy, such as discrimination of imports through tariffs and other impediments to trade, may motivate direct investment as a substitute for imports.
- Marketing may be more effective from a base within the host economy and may again motivate direct investment as a substitute for imports.
- Oligopolistic reaction, owing to the competition between rival firms.
- Product cycle, explaining how the various factors given above may interact over time to determine the effectiveness of activities in different locations.

3 Sources of advantages over licensing:[2]
- Secrecy and novelty of technology increases the gain of internalizing it through direct investment.

- The size and stability of the market, generally making direct investment a more attractive alternative since it increases the likelihood that the sunk costs can be covered.
- Government policy, making direct investment more competitive if predictable.

Concerning the last category, riskiness in operations reduces the attractiveness of direct investment to licensing. All in all, firm and country characteristics interact to determine whether direct investment pays. Crucial country characteristics may be, for example, factor costs, geographic location in relation to markets for input or output goods, the quality of infrastructure, the size and growth of the host country's market, taxes, regulations and other host country policies. Concerning firm or industry characteristics, high labour intensity makes wage costs crucial, transport costs have a considerable bearing on location, pollution intensity makes the level of environmental protection matter and so forth. Robinson (1987) discusses how trading costs, factor costs and social/political costs have to be taken into consideration as a firm determines the comparative advantage of countries relative to each link in its value added chain.

This study is generally not concerned with the firm characteristics that determine the profitability of direct investment. We simply conclude that the undertaking of direct investment requires that an MNE expects either to retain larger benefits or account for smaller costs compared with the best alternative. However, we do need some idea of how host countries are affected by direct investment. This is discussed in the following section.

THE SOCIO-ECONOMIC IMPACT ON HOST COUNTRIES

This study is confined to the socio-economic impact of foreign direct investment on developing host economies. The socio-economic impact encompasses, in principle, all the effects that can be identified, quantified and monetized. As pointed out by Lall and Streeten (1977), however, there are limitations to the socio-economic analysis. For example, a general distinction cannot be made between preferences on grounds of their social and ethical desirability, and factors that shape preferences cannot be taken into account. Effects on the distribution of income within host countries are also not dealt with satisfactorily. These distributional effects are merely noted in the following.

Traditionally, the contribution of capital was stressed for all kinds of foreign investment. Direct investment is naturally a source of long-term financing. However, a host country may be able, for example, to borrow internationally and foster domestic firms instead. A comparison of direct investment with indirect or portfolio investment is therefore appropriate. When borrowing, a creditor country has immediate control over the usage of funds. If debt servicing becomes difficult, it finds itself constrained and subject to a repayment schedule which is unrelated to its economy. With direct investment, the funds provided are controlled by an MNE, which runs the risk of failure. The firm-specific advantages of that firm are the real contribution of direct investment. While profitability in financial terms is assured in theory, the impact on the host economy hinges on the extent to ‘which rents spill over to domestic agents.

As noted, privileged financing should not be the crucial oligopolistic advantage that motivates direct investment. Moreover, MNEs often avoid the exposure of more capital than necessary to exchange risk in poor countries. Some countries restrict opportunities of MNEs to bring in capital and encourage funding of direct investment within the host economy. The consequences are discussed by Lall and Streeten (1977). Nevertheless, the possible contribution of capital, not least in the form of indirect effects, is important to the host economy. Other kinds of investment such as aid and portfolio investment may be spurred. Domestic savings, on the other hand, are often argued to be discouraged by capital inflows (Papanek 1972; Areskoug 1973; Fry 1984). Gupta and Islam (1983) found that direct investment has had a favourable impact on savings in Asian countries, although the causal linkages are doubtful (see also Lee *et al* 1986).

Whether direct investment contributes capital to the host economy is a matter subordinate to the question of how the balance of payments is affected. The net effect hinges on the inflows and outflows of capital, as well as the effects on the current account. Since an MNE carries the risk of failure, it usually requires a risk premium which would make a country's expected cost of obtaining foreign exchange through direct investment higher than that through borrowing. Concerning the current account, direct investment tends to stimulate exports and/or substitute imports. In addition, MNEs may curtail the growth of barriers to trade in home countries, to the benefit of domestic firms.[3] Taken together, such influences may outweigh the cost of repatriation of profits, improve the balance of payments and give rise to an overall economic expansion. On the other hand, MNEs are often more dependent than domestic firms on imported inputs, so that a positive effect on the current account cannot be taken for granted.

Today, it is widely recognized that the most powerful effects of direct investment are associated with the transfer of organizational practices, management and technology to the host country (cf. Caves 1982). Benefits are likely to accrue owing to spin-off effects on domestic factors of production. This may take place through, for example, the turnover of trained personnel, forward and backward linkages, demonstration effects and even government officials who come into contact with MNEs. Concerning the transfer of technology, benefits are likely to arise because MNEs are the prime innovators and the most efficient in realizing the potential of new technology. However, costs may arise because MNEs use monopolistic power, and the administrative weaknesses of host countries, to import 'too poor' technology at 'too high' a price. This may occur because MNEs maximize their global profits rather than those of individual subsidiaries.

Direct investment may make a net addition to the productive resources of the host economy, or there may be a crowding out of domestic activities. With MNEs substituting for domestic firms, or influencing their technology, it is thus important how foreign technology compares with domestic. In general, it is more capital intensive in developing countries. A replacement of domestic firms by foreign firms may then make capital more scarce. In the presence of a common distortion in the domestic price of capital, Batra (1986) demonstrated immiserizing growth in a developing host country owing to direct investment when little capital is brought in and more labour intensive domestic firms are crowded out.

One important aspect of the impact on domestic industry concerns market structure. It is often argued that the entrance of foreign firms reduces the market concentration in the host economy. On the other hand, the sheer size of foreign-owned subsidiaries, their capacity to tackle bureaucracies, use of predatory pricing etc. may instead lead to the establishment of monopolies, particularly in protected or segmented markets (see Lall 1979, Blomström 1983). Moran (1985) discusses effects on market concentration in both directions. The substitution of foreign-owned monopolies for domestic monopolies is detrimental to the host economy since profits are repatriated rather than invested locally. Another related danger is suppression of domestic entrepreneurship. A weak national entrepreneurial class may be taken over by MNEs and relegated to a subordinate role as a provider of ancillary inputs (Lall and Streeten 1977).

Finally, there may be various external effects on the social, cultural, political and physical environment in the host country. In his later work, Hymer (1960) maintained that MNEs, partly through their superior ability to store, retrieve and process information, exert a considerable impact on the social, cultural and political conditions in poor countries. Hymer's view of the role of MNEs in this context was strongly critical, but both positive and negative influence are conceivable. In any case, such effects cannot be recorded in terms of social values, since they concern the very transformation of such values and are therefore excluded in this study.

Physical effects on the environment, however, can be valued, at least in principle. Environmental effects may be of great importance, not only because of their impact on the welfare of the host country, but also because they matter for the establishment of direct investment in the first place. Walter (1972) and Pearson (1976) predicted a substantial relocation of pollution intensive activities from countries with higher control costs to those with lower ones. Since we can expect a stricter regulation of environmental effects in the industrialized countries in the future, this factor may become increasingly important. We return to this matter in Chapter 4.

To sum up, both positive and negative effects of investment can be expected on host economies. Transfers of capital, organization, management, technology and so forth are likely to give rise to rents that MNEs cannot capture, raising the productivity of domestic factors. Meanwhile, there are costs due to, for example, repatriation of profits, the monopolistic power of MNEs, the crowding out of domestic firms and negative external effects. This exposition merely illustrates the complexity of the impact, and that different agents, such as firms, workers and consumers, are likely to be differently affected.

In addition, as is central to this work, we have the host country government. Corporate income tax and other tax payments represent one of the most tangible gains of a host country from foreign direct investment. The government matters in another sense as well. Owing to its sovereign power over its jurisdiction, it is in a unique position to influence how direct investment affects the host economy. For example, the government may forbid direct investment in the first place, subsidize certain costs, impose performance requirements or, in the extreme, nationalize a foreign-owned firm. It may be asked whether this capacity on the part of the host country government is a curse or a blessing.

THE BASIC MOTIVATION OF MULTINATIONAL ENTERPRISES AND HOST COUNTRIES

MNEs are normally large firms, vertically and/or horizontally integrated across nation states, which act according to global strategies. Their internal needs may differ considerably from the market forces to which atomistic companies relate. Knickerbocker (1973) and Vernon (1983) described how MNEs may enter markets 'clump-wise', i.e. either none or all competitors invest in a country. Sölvell (1987) speaks of strategic behaviour on two levels, the national and the international. De la Torre and Neckar (1988) distinguish between factors which relate to the 'global strategy' of MNEs, including synergetic or competitive contributions to other units, and those that relate to the investment climate of specific countries. We do not make this distinction explicit, but view MNEs as maximizing their overall profits. This may or may not be equivalent to maximizing the profits of individual subsidiaries. Understanding specific MNEs should, of course, require a more precise formulation of strategies.

Host countries, on the other hand, may be governed by, for example, cultural, political and institutional factors. Politicians may well take their personal gains into consideration, favouring, for example, tax revenues, bribes and the welfare of influential groups. Nevertheless they can be expected to weigh personal motives against other interests. Without any ambition to explain everything, this work is confined to socio-economic motives for host country behaviour *vis-à-vis* direct investment. Thus, we abstain from a public choice approach and assume that governments act in the interest of the inhabitants they represent. Other possibilities are commented on when this appears to be most appropriate.

MNEs and host countries are thought of as negotiating a division of the economic gains from direct investment. To illustrate what is open for bargaining from a subsidiary run under foreign ownership, consider the following representation of gains (which essentially is used throughout the study). The utility C_u of the host country can be written as a function

$$C_u = C_u\,(\phi\pi + \Phi,\, G,\, B) \qquad (2.1)$$

where ϕ is the corporate income tax rate, π is the profit before tax, Φ is a lump-sum tax, G represents positive external effects and B represents negative external effects. G stands for 'goods' and B for 'bads'. Furthermore, assume that the utility function of the host country is constantly increasing in goods and constantly decreasing in bads over the intervals dealt with. Given that monetary values can be determined for the external effects, we can express the discounted gain of the host country as a money value, rewriting (2.1) as

$$u_C = \phi\pi + \Phi + X_G - X_B \qquad (2.2)$$

where X_G is a function of G and X_B is a function of B. Assume also that the home country's tax system is such that the host country's tax rate matters to the MNE, which is generally realistic. As discussed in the next section, this is the case with a tax exemption system in the home country. We write the discounted gain of the MNE as

$$u_F = (1 - \phi) \pi - \Phi \qquad (2.3)$$

which states that the MNE earns the profit not paid in income tax minus lump-sum taxes. As can be seen, there is a trade-off in the gain of the MNE and the host country. Given that the value of production can be taken for granted, i.e. that policies affect only the distribution of costs and benefits (given that production occurs), the outcome can be illustrated by a 'goods–bads box' (Figure 2.1). Value added and positive external effects are depicted on the horizontal axis, and negative external effects are shown on the vertical. The net value of the project is given by the width of the box minus the height.

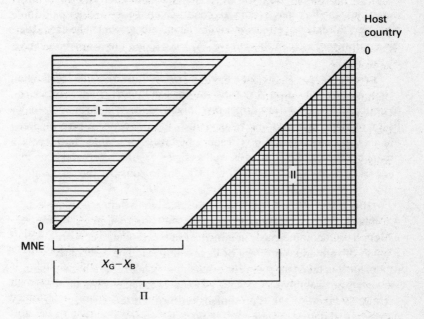

Figure 2.1 The goods–bads box of an investment project

Any division of gains is represented by a certain point within the box, with the gain of the MNE given by the horizontal minus the vertical distance from the lower left-hand corner. The gain of the host country is measured reversely from the upper right-hand corner, with the utility of goods given by the horizontal distance to the left and the disutility of bads by the vertical downwards. The MNE does not accept an outcome in I, which is the area above the 45° diagonal from the MNE corner, since it then pays higher compensation for bads than it earns in profit net of tax. Similarly, the host country does not accept an outcome in II. This leaves us with the mid-corridor open for negotiation – in which both the MNE and the host country make a real gain.

The interval π along the lower boundary of the box marks what can be achieved by a corporate income tax alone, since external effects by definition accrue to the host country. The outcome can be somewhere else only if Φ serves as a compensation to the host country for accepting a negative external effect or to the MNE for causing a positive external effect. In practice, external effects are seldom taxed effectively in developing countries. Since they are not internalized by an MNE (it is simply rewarded or paid for if compensation is realized in any direction), the box may seem redundant. Even if they are not paid for, however, the external effects should be taken into account. The candidate for equilibrium is then the interval $X_G - X_B$ along the lower boundary of the box.

The usefulness of the goods–bads box is limited in at least four respects. First, taxation is not the only possible host country measure to appropriate gains from direct investment. Second, information may be incomplete and asymmetrical. Third, the effects of a project, i.e. the size and shape of the box, cannot be taken for granted but depend on the behaviour of countries as well as firms. Fourth, costs and benefits vary over time, which makes it insufficient to consider the discounted value of goods and bads.

In this study, these limitations are relaxed in certain crucial aspects. As made clear, we take into account the host country's option to nationalize. Incompleteness in information is considered concerning the pay-off of individual projects or host countries. The discounted value of a project is taken as given for a subsidiary under foreign ownership. However, profitability may decline subsequent to nationalization. Finally, account is taken of the time dimension through the distinction made between the stages *ex ante* and *ex post* the set-up of a subsidiary. In the next section we look more closely at the behavioural options open to MNEs and host countries.

BEHAVIOURAL OPTIONS OF MULTINATIONAL ENTERPRISES AND HOST COUNTRIES

Agents should be expected to do the best they can at each point in time, which follows from the requirement of perfectness. The crucial distinction in time in the MNE–host country relationship is between the *ex ante* and *ex post* stages of setting up a subsidiary. In the intial stage of an investment project, an MNE incurs costs in terms of investment, development, technology and know-how transfers. Except for expenditures on non-transportable and non-convertible plant and equipment, these concern the development of new contacts, habits and ways of doing things which are necessary for a subsidiary to be operational in a certain foreign environment. Once operations have been established, costs fall and benefits accrue. If a project is undertaken, it must be expected that the *ex post* profit at least compensates for the initial costs.

If an MNE establishes a subsidiary by incurring expenditure sunk in the project, it may thereby weaken its bargaining position *vis-à-vis* the host country. Of course, the host country can realize payments to an MNE *ex ante*, which we refer to as initial incentives. Subsequent to the set-up of a subsidiary, there are essentially three possible strategies for a host country.[4]

1 It may act as agreed *ex ante*.
2 It may not interfere with ownership but impose performance requirements, raise tax rates or provide economic incentives etc. We refer to any such activities, which aim at determining or influencing the behaviour of an MNE, as 'taxation'.
3 It may undertake forced divestment, i.e. take over the ownership and control of a subsidiary, which is referred to as 'nationalization'.[5]

A one-time division of the goods–bads box, as discussed in the preceding section, may be taken for granted under binding international law. However, this is not the case when nations are sovereign. Throughout this study, the existence of *ex ante* agreements is neglected, since they are not realized anyway unless they constitute the options that are optimal *ex post*. Thus, we are left with taxation and nationalization. Beginning with the latter, we can identify a scale of host country interference with ownership. In line with Hood and Young (1979), the possible arrangements can be ordered in terms of ascending interference:

● no ownership participation – subsidiaries are wholly foreign-owned;
● joint ventures – MNEs share ownership with local firms;
● licensing agreements;
● technical assistance agreements;

- industrial co-operation
- rejection of direct investment in the first place, or nationalization when a project has been set up

For simplicity, in this study we consider only the extreme alternatives of none or complete interference, with the latter referred to as nationalization. Although the direct objective may vary, nationalization can in general be thought of as a measure to prevent repatriation of profits abroad, which implies that the aim is short-term gains. An alternative objective is to break up foreign market power, in case the purpose is long-term gains. This is not believed to be the general case, however. The observation that selective nationalization tends to be associated with acute economic difficulties in host countries supports this view. See Chapters 5–7 for further discussions.

Turning to taxation, the policies belonging in this category concern the following:

- repatriation of profits;
- purchase of inputs locally and abroad;
- sales domestically and abroad;
- the prices used by an MNE, including royalty payments etc;
- employment, local participation in various activities and training of local personnel;
- the transfer of technology, including establishment of research and development (R & D)activities;
- credit policies;
- degree of competition
- environmental and social protection

As with nationalization, we assume that the host country's objective is to retain profits that would otherwise be repatriated. The actual policy may take the form of an income tax, subsidy, regulation, performance requirement regarding employment, technology, trade etc., an informal hint and so forth. Of course, any interference with the behaviour of an MNE may, in practice, influence its effectiveness. Reduced burdens and restrictions may boost the productivity of a subsidiary to the advantage of both MNE and host country. On the other hand, host country policies which adjust for market imperfections may increase the social value of direct investment without causing an MNE too much damage. Performance requirements often aim to stimulate positive external effects etc. However, this study is concerned with the broad developments in taxation and nationalization of MNE affiliates rather than the specific design of policies. Therefore we simplify by viewing the profit under viewing the profit under foreign ownership as given and independent of the level of taxation, provided that production occurs.

Neither nationalization nor taxation should be an issue unless there is potential benefit to capture. However, if a host country does pursue either policy, it has to consider the possible response of the MNE targeted, as well as possible responses by other agents.

DIRECT AND INDIRECT EFFECTS

There are basically two kinds of effects which can be distinguished in response to taxation or nationalization by a host country – direct and indirect effects. Both generally take the form of costs. It can be noted that, throughout, we associate one MNE with one investment project. The two kinds of effects can be described as follows.

Direct effects relate to the MNE against which a host country takes action. Faced with taxation, an MNE may (a) continue to operate as it otherwise would, (b) withdraw completely without producing or (c) continue to operate but adapt to host country action through transfer pricing, reducing operations to a minimum, altering the quality of output etc. An MNE's ability to choose the second or third responses cannot be generalized across firms. It will depend on the opportunities available to produce elsewhere, the flexibility and nature of technology, the relationship between affiliate and parent company etc. In any case, these responses can be expected to impose costs on an MNE, which must be weighed against the costs of complying with taxation.

Faced with nationalization by a host country, which cuts off an affiliate from the ownership and technology of the parent company, an MNE is considered to be unable to retaliate. It must organize a possible defence in advance, either by not investing *ex ante* or by making a subsidiary dependent on the parent company so that output falls subsequent to takeover.[6] Clearly, nationalization is not a viable alternative for all investment projects. The minimum requirement for a successful nationalization policy is that the profit under domestic ownership is larger than the share of the profit under foreign ownership which can be retained by the host country through taxation.

It is impossible to generalize about a host country's ability to generate and withold profits under domestic ownership. The metal or stone in a mine or the trees in a forest are easily captured, as are buildings, physical machinery and stocks. Some of the services and skills of the personnel within a subsidiary may also be possible to capture. However, assets within the parent company, or those that are realized only through the interaction between parent and affiliate, are inaccessible, and the question arises as to what extent the host country can substitute for them. For these reasons, nationalization tends to deprive an affiliate of a certain amount of management, technology, distribution networks abroad, brand names etc. This is likely to depress a nationalized affiliate's pre-tax profitability and the positive external effects on the host country.

Nevertheless, there are undoubtedly many potentially profitable projects which could also generate substantial profits under domestic ownership. It is their possible nationalization which is at stake here. The theoretical analysis will not be concerned with the fact that the likelihood of nationalization is greater in natural resource extraction, utilities or highly standardized manufacturing than in activities whose profitability hinges on advanced technology and the export channels of parent companies.

Indirect effects relate to other agents than those targeted by the MNE. We distinguish between the following kinds:

1 Military retaliation by home countries. As seen in Chapter 1, 'gun-boat diplomacy', mainly expropriation of customs' houses and other military actions, constituted a real threat well into the twentieth century. Overt military action seems to have ceased today, but covert action cannot be ruled out.
2 Economic responses by home country governments, multilateral organizations or other official agents. Economic retaliation by industrialized countries or multilateral organizations such as the World Bank has attracted much attention. It is less often noted that there may also be responses by other host countries.
3 An impact on direct or portfolio investment, which is associated with the *ex ante* investment decision of other MNEs than that targeted, or the lending decisions of banks and other private creditor institutions.

Military retaliation can today be considered a small threat in response to selective nationalizations, since it is costly for home countries. Moreover, it is the response which most dramatizes the MNE–host country relationship. Economic responses are, by contrast, frequent. The importance of inter-state relationships for direct investment has been much debated over the years. Gilpin (1975) maintained that direct investment requires political backing, and is therefore dependent on the supremacy of a hegemonic power. This was disputed by McCloskey (1971) and Keohane and Nye (1977), who pointed out that shifts in hegemonic power do not fully account for past policy shifts and that portfolio investment has not been threatened at the same time as direct investment. Host country behaviour would not depend on the opportunities for retaliation by the home country, but governments would be able to manage conflicts without a hierarchical relationship. The arguments can be questioned, however. Can a state commit itself to abstain from action which is in its interest? And if it is in a country's interest to abstain from action, why would it have to commit itself? In practice, countries are intimately related through flows of goods and factors between them. In this study we take the actions of countries and organizations into consideration only to the extent that they materialize in effects on direct or portfolio investment.

Consider first the possibility of indirect effects on direct investment. Williamson (1986) and Tirole (1986), for example, argue that the fear of appropriation discourages investment, while Milgrom and Roberts (1990) observe that it encourages parties to waste resources by investing in their bargaining position. However, theoretical studies that seek to demonstrate these results tend to make simplistic assumptions. For example, any deviation from an announced strategy has been taken to destroy a country's reputation for ever, and to reduce future investment flows to zero. Empirical studies, in contrast, have come up with inconclusive results. Green's (1972) study of the inter-country pattern of marketing investment and Thunnell's (1977) study of intra-country flows over time found that there were no significant negative effects from nationalization on direct investment. Although Kobrin (1982) in a study of MNEs from within found that MNEs maintain that host country policies matter he found little factual evidence that they actually do. Work on the impact of environmental policies has similarly found only scattered evidence of effects on investment decisions. Among studies that do find an impact, Guisinger (1985) demonstrated effects of performance requirements and investment incentives.

The fairly weak empirical evidence for effects of host country policies on the flows of direct investment may not be surprising. As pointed out by Eaton and Gersovitz (1984), nationalization need not occur to exert an impact. Given a reasonable amount of foresight and rationality within MNEs, the prospects of the policy prevent the undertaking of direct investment in the first place. Moreover, the complexity of the asset portfolio of MNEs may make it difficult to verify changes in the flows of direct investment, which may be realized through inconspicuous adjustment. Finally, the sensitivity of direct investment to host country behaviour may vary considerably among firms and countries.

The size of the gains that a host country can acquire from a major project basically depends on its investment opportunities in relation to those of other countries. UNCTC (1988) points out that many countries may have difficulties in attracting direct investment irrespective of their policies. Those countries tend to be small, and have negative or low growth and an adverse location. Other countries which are more favourably endowed may attract a great deal of direct investment even when they treat MNEs relatively adversely. There is nothing controversial about these observations. Our concern is the interdependence of the behaviour of different countries. Host country policies cannot be fully understood by studying countries in isolation.

The present work is confined to the interdependence of host countries in their interaction with MNEs. However, some comments on the home countries of these firms may be appropriate. One aspect of their behaviour *vis-à-vis* MNEs which has attracted a great deal of attention in the last few years is the tax treatment of residents' foreign source income. There are different kinds of tax systems, although most countries attempt to avoid double taxation. Under the territorial approach, foreign source income is not taxed at all. Some European countries, including France and the Netherlands, use such a system. Under the more common residence approach, the home country taxes foreign source income but may grant a deduction for taxes paid in the host country. Some countries exempt foreign income received by residents from their own tax including retained earnings of foreign subsidiaries, which allows capital-exporting taxes to be deferred until income is repatriated to the investor in the form of dividends.

The crediting of corporate taxes in home countries is important to the design of corporate tax in host countries. The host country's corporate income tax aims at witholding equity accruing to foreigners. If the home country uses resident-based taxation with deduction for foreign taxes, a tax cut in the host country is of no value to an MNE, but merely transfers income from the capital-importing country to the capital-exporting country. With a territorial approach, however, the host country's corporate income tax affects the MNE directly. The situation is the same with an exempt tax system under which foreign earned income is tax exempt at home if foreign tax has been paid.

Most important home countries with residential tax systems have some element of tax exemption. The US tax system, for example, has a deferral provision which allows firms to report foreign earned income when repatriating after foreign taxes have been paid rather than when it is earned. In case firms do not repatriate but reward domestic shareholders via capital gains instead of dividends (for foreign earned income), the tax system is in effect equivalent to an exempt tax system. Revisions in the 1980s have led to a less favourable treatment of foreign source income than used to be the case.[7] Meanwhile, US direct investment abroad has declined markedly from 1981, while direct investment in the United States has increased substantially. In this study, however, we assume an exempt tax system throughout, so that the host country's tax does matter for an MNE.[8] This is valid as a generalization of the real world.

Concerning the indirect effects on portfolio investment, it should be noted that the bulk of formalization and modelling of political and economic risks has occurred in response to the rapid increase in international bank lending to developing countries during the last 15 years.[9] Nationalization and other host country actions which affect foreign investors adversely run the risk of damaging a country's ability to borrow in the international credit markets. Empirical evidence has shown that spreads in interest rates do not respond very significantly to the usual indicators of creditworthiness. (Edwards 1984; Hajivassiliou 1986). However, the important role of credit rationing is clear. If a country's opportunity to borrow commercially is depressed, foreign exchange must be obtained from other, less favourable, sources.

THE THEORY OF THE OBSOLESCING BARGAIN

In this section we briefly discuss the theory of a 'changing balance of power' or the 'theory of the obsolescing bargain'. This has represented the predominant view of the MNE–host country relationship for more than a decade. Some empirical developments which seem at odds with the theory are pointed out.

According to the idea of a changing balance of power, which goes back to Vernon (1971) and Moran (1974), the distribution of bargaining power between MNEs and host countries shifts to the advantage of the latter over time. This can be explained at both the project level and the country level. We have already noted that direct investment requires sunk costs to begin with, while benefits accrue to an investing firm subsequent to the establishment of a subsidiary. This is in contrast with the host country, which first receives benefits but later incurs costs in the form of capital outflows. Thus, an MNE becomes more susceptible to host country pressure for gains over time. Meanwhile, the development process increases countries' access to foreign markets and technology. This improves their capacity to run firms under domestic ownership and enables them to put pressure on foreign-controlled subsidiaries for a greater share of the gains.

Although there are alternative views, stressing the potential of mutual profits for firms and countries, the theory of the obsolescing bargain has attracted considerable attention. The implication is that the expected profitability of direct investment would decline in developing countries, as would the flow of investment. However, it was argued in Chapter 1 that there is no simple relationship between host country policies and direct investment.

Minor (1987) pointed out that the flow of direct investment increased in the mid-1970s, when nationalization peaked, and thereafter declined as nationalization became less frequent. But what is the causal relationship? If direct investment is reversely related to nationalization, why did it increase in 1975? If nationalization is positively related to the flow of direct investment, why did the developing countries not nationalize to a greater extent that they did in 1978–9? A comparison of the flow of direct investment and the number of nationalizations across regions further indicates that there is no clear-cut relationship.[10] As discussed in the preceding section, this has already been concluded in empirical studies.

The developments in host country policies seem to fit the theory of the obsolescing bargain up to the mid-1970s, but what about after that period? Could more benevolent host country policies have been a response to an expectation of reduced investment flows, in turn caused by expectations of adverse host country policies if the flows continued on a grand scale? Such reasoning seems difficult to support, since the matter of which expectations came first is obscure, or, at any rate, impossible to verify. The factual evidence does not point towards a reduction in direct investment prior to the shift towards more benevolent host country policies. The picture must be regarded as incomplete, which signals that there are anomalies in the mainstream conception of the MNE–host country relationship.

A note is appropriate here regarding the argument that the change in host country behaviour from the mid-1970s, including the termination of nationalization, merely reflects a change in attitudes. The developing countries have been said to convert to 'an acceptance of the likelihood of mutually beneficial co-operation . . . . The possible contribution to economic development and the transfer of technology has been generally recognized in developing countries' (UNCTC 1988: 262). Clearly, there has been a broader change in political perceptions at national levels in the direction of more liberal market ideologies. This is not to say, however, that the policy change would somehow not reflect economic rationality. Again, it is our point of departure that host country policies can be understood on the basis of economic costs and benefits.

THE MARKET FOR DIRECT INVESTMENT

It is now time to sum up the arguments which form the basis of this work. Our point of departure is that direct investment is traded in a market where it is supplied by firms and demanded by countries. The concept of a market implies that a good or service is traded at a certain price. The 'goods' can be characterized as the effects generated by investment projects. The 'price' is, in principle, the share of the gains acquired by host countries. But what is the level of the price, and how is it determined?

The notion of a market has seldom been made explicit in past work on direct investment, and there has not been much clarification of its characteristics. In the market for direct investment, there is certainly no perfect competition, neither between countries nor between firms. Nor, generally speaking are there monopolies. The bulk of direct investment is undertaken by a fairly small number of MNEs – between 300 and 600. Even though there are many small and medium-sized MNEs, less than five tend to dominate most industries. Meanwhile, the stock of foreign direct investment is highly concentrated, particularly in manufacturing, where six to seven countries host some three-quarters of the total stock in developing countries.

The market for direct investment looks different for the two major kinds of direct investment. Import-substituting or 'tariff-jumping' direct investment is generated by impediments to exports from another country. Export-oriented direct investment takes advantage of low factor costs, which outweigh the transport costs of shipping to and from a host country. The difference between the two categories is fairly sharp in manufacturing, although some investment in the former may switch to the latter over time. It is less straightforward to classify investment in natural resource extraction along these lines. Such investment is often oriented towards exports, whether final processing occurs here or elsewhere. However, its objective is to make efficient use of resources which are inherent to the host economy.

In the case of import-substituting investment, MNEs can in principle invest in every country – but do not substitute investment in one country for that in another. The bargaining power of countries can be expected to be great, since they may play off firms against each other for shares of their markets. In the case of export-oriented investment, MNEs can choose between countries, which accounts for the weak bargaining position of the latter. This leads to the perhaps surprising conclusion that host countries have a greater ability to extract rents from import-substituting investment than from export-oriented investment. In no way does this in fact contradict the view that the former is less favourable for social welfare (cf. Johnson 1967; Bhagwati 1978; Kojima and Ozawa 1984). Import-substituting investment tends to be generated by artificial barriers to trade, such as tariffs and non-tariff barriers. With trade displaced, there may well be less efficient resource allocation and a smaller or even negative net gain to divide. Export-oriented investment, however, expands trade and implies a more efficient allocation of resources. The net gain to be distributed is likely to be larger from this kind of investment.

Which kind of investment that has the largest potential for the future is a question for debate. With a possible escalation of the barriers to trade, the future of export-oriented investment may be in danger. On the other hand, the inter-country differences in factor costs will in that case widen, requiring increasing policy distortions to prevent a diffusion of production. Increased robotization may lessen the attractiveness of low labour costs, but it is unlikely to erase it altogether. Import-substituting investment has suffered from the sluggish growth and accumulation of debt burdens in developing countries. However, the rate of growth is generally high in developing countries compared with industrialized countries – a state of affairs which may be expected to continue. Thus, there should be a considerable potential for future direct investment in both categories. As seen in Chapter 1, official forecasts today lean towards an investment revival in the developing countries.

For export-oriented investment, obtaining gains involves competition with other potential host countries. The same is true for investment which targets a group of markets (including that of the host country), and to some extent for import-substituting investment as well. With limited capacity, MNEs generally invest 'in one country at a time'. Moreover, the developing countries' persistent scarcity of factors that MNEs have in ample supply, such as capital, technology, management skills etc., suggest a competitive edge for MNEs. Competition between host countries can be observed in, for example, preferential treatment of foreign firms and initial incentives. The existence of 'tax havens' is another conspicuous example of host country competition. The tax haven fraction of world-wide pre-tax earnings of US controlled affiliates rose from 11 to 20 per cent over the period 1968–82 (Hines 1987).

Despite the importance of host country competition, it has been examined in only a few studies. Doyle and van Wijnbergen (1984), who analysed taxation by competing host countries, is a rare exception. However, their results hinge on the assumption of zero profits owing to perfect competition between firms. As pointed out by Caves (1982), direct investment often generates high returns on intra-marginal units of investment because subsidiaries draw on parent firms' intangible assets, or excess capacity in tangible assets. In a market where both countries and firms compete, there is no justification for assuming zero profits after tax.

Assuming zero profits means neglecting the distribution of gains as well as the question whether direct investment is undertaken in the first place. The consideration of one firm–one country interaction neglects competition between firms as well as countries. Instead, this work starts out from the assumption that there are potentially profitable investment projects. Different host countries compete to obtain those projects and acquire as much as possible of the gains. In order to do that they may have a range of alternative policy options, represented here by taxation and nationalization.

With a potential for mutual profits from an investment project, maximization of overall welfare requires that it is undertaken. However, an MNE invests only to the extent that its expected return is higher than that of its best alternative. Building on (2.3), the requirement for a firm to undertake direct investment f in country i can be written

$$f \text{ in } i \text{ iff:} \geq E\left[[(1 - \phi_i)\pi_i - \Phi_i](1 - r_i) - S_i\right] \geq$$
$$\max \left(E\left[[(1 - \phi_j)\pi_j - \Phi_j](1 - r_j) - S_j\right], 0\right)$$
$$j \neq i \tag{2.4}$$

where π is the profit before tax, ϕ is the corporate income tax, Φ is a lump-sum tax and S is the sunk cost of setting up a subsidiary. Expression (2.4) says that a firm weighs its expected profit net of tax with the probability of not being nationalized, i.e. $1 - r$. Investment is undertaken in country i if and only if the expected profit net of tax is positive and larger than in the best alternative host country j. The best alternative other than direct investment in another host country, whether production at home, licensing, joint ventures etc., is set at zero.

The attractiveness of the best alternative depends on the anticipated behaviour of other potential host countries. A host country's maximization problem can be written

$$\max_{\phi, \Phi, \lambda} \sum_{t=1}^{\infty} \sum_{f=1}^{n_t} \left[(1 - \lambda_f)(\phi_{ft}\pi_{ft} + \Phi_{ft} + X_{Gft} - X_{Bft}) + \lambda_f(\pi_{ft}^N + X_{Gft}^N - X_{Bft}^N)\right]$$

$$\text{subject to } f \text{ in } i, \phi_f \in [0, 1] \text{ and } \lambda_f \in \{0, 1\} \tag{2.5}$$

which can be compared with (2.2). The host country maximizes its gains, over an infinite time horizon and a potential flow of n investment projects each period, through corporate income tax ϕ, lump-sum taxes Φ and nationalization λ. It is assumed that the policies of a host country are able to discriminate perfectly between firms. When an affiliate is nationalized, the whole profit is retained by the host country but the level of profit as well as the external effects may be affected. The levels subsequent to nationalization are indicated by superscript N, The corporate income tax is a continuous variable between zero and unity, and nationalization is discrete, taking a value of either zero or unity (nationalization). Expressions (2.4) and (2.5) represent the two sides of the market, on each of which a number of agents maximize their gains from direct investment over time.

Finally, we consider that potential host countries, like MNEs, tend to be heterogeneous. The 'goods' traded in the market are diversified, and the value depends on which seller and buyer strike a deal. This seems to imply that the determination of the 'price' is complex. Hajivassiliou (1987), in his study of the debt repayment problems of poor countries, incorporated country heterogeneity through an error-components structure which deviated from the standard stochastic properties. Here, dissimilarities between countries will systematically influence the behavioural options of MNEs and host countries.

SUMMARY

In this chapter we have presented a theoretical background to MNE–host country interaction. The view of MNEs adopted is that provided by the OLI framework. We assume that both MNEs and host countries maximize their profits and socio-economic gains respectively from direct investment within a bargaining framework. Each side acts as best it can at each point in time. The crucial distinction in time is that between the *ex ante* and *ex post* stages of undertaking a project. The reason is that the establishment of a subsidiary imposes costs on an MNE while benefits accrue later. *Ex post* the set-up of a project, a host country seeks to capture as much as possible of the gains through taxation or nationalization. The direct effects of these policies are defined as those relating to the MNE targeted. The indirect effects relate to other agents, notably private agents contemplating to undertake direct or portfolio investment. Home country behaviour is not explicitly considered, but an exempt tax system is assumed to prevail at home. Accordingly, the host countries' tax rates matter to MNEs.

It is argued that the mainstream theory of a 'changing balance of power', or 'the theory of the obsolescing bargain', does not explain the major developments in host country behaviour in the last decade. This calls for a partly new framework of analysis. We view direct investment as traded in a market where it is supplied by firms and demanded by countries. The share of the gains acquired by host countries can be interpreted as the 'price'. The characteristics of the market differ between, for example, direct investment which substitutes for imports and that which is export oriented. Competition between host countries is relatively more important for the latter kind. In Chapters 3–7 we investigate the consequences of competition between host countries through taxation and nationalization.

Part II

Taxation of multinational enterprise affiliates

3 Taxation of multinational enterprise affiliates by competing host countries

INTRODUCTION

In this chapter we are concerned with taxation of MNEs when there are competing potential host countries. The analysis is most relevant for export-oriented manufacturing affiliates rather than for import-substituting investment, for which competition between firms is relatively more important. Nationalization is ruled out, meaning that internalization of activities within MNEs is taken for granted. This is partly motivated by the fact that nationalization is not an issue for all direct investment, whereas taxation is. In particular, nationalization does not often pose a threat to export-oriented investment where the parent's access to foreign markets tends to be crucial. Furthermore, complete information is assumed to prevail throughout. Applications to the real world will require adjustments for firm and industry-specific conditions, including imperfections in information.

The fundamental objective of taxation is normally to generate government revenue in the least distorting way. This motivates uniform tax rates on capital goods in closed economies. As expounded in the literature on optimal taxation (e.g. Diamond and Mirrlees 1971), it is inefficient to have firms within and across industries facing different relative prices in factors of production.[1] The case for uniform tax rates looks different when international aspects are considered, however. In fact, corporate tax rates vary considerably across countries, from not much more than zero in 'tax paradises' to about 50 per cent in countries such as France, Germany and Canada. Although there are cultural and constitutional explanations, the significance of economic explanations is evident. Tax policy must pay attention to a country's competitive situation, or the tax sensitivity of capital flows. For growth and economic development in general, it is a prerequisite for a country to attract investment. At the same time, a government wants to extract gains from business, particularly from foreign direct investment, whose profits net of tax are sooner or later repatriated abroad.

As discussed in Chapter 2, we assume an exempt tax system in the home country. The host country faces a trade-off between raising taxes and attracting direct investment. The task of negotiating a mutually rewarding contract between an MNE and a host country is complicated by the time dimension. Because direct investment is associated with fixed and irreversible costs, its undertaking requires that the MNE can expect to repatriate a profit which is higher than the variable cost. With more than one jurisdiction involved, however, agents can not commit their future behaviour. On the contrary, 'perfectness' ensures that an agent does not stick to a contract when he can do better. In other words, contracts are bound to be broken unless it is optimal to keep them. An MNE invests only if a satisfactory profit can be expected, given optimal host country behaviour.

Given complete information, it is well known that in the one firm–one country case direct investment is prevented by the prospect of optimal host country taxation. Regardless of what is negotiated *ex ante*, the host country taxes the whole profit *ex post* (see, for example, Shenfeld 1984). In accordance with Kydland and Prescott (1977), the optimal plan of the host country is dynamically inconsistent, and the outcome is socially suboptimal since potential mutual gains are forgone. The country would gain if it could pre-commit itself to abstain from the optimal *ex post* policy. This is a special case of the problem of underinvestment due to opportunism analysed by Williamson (1975). At the same time, plenty of direct investment can be observed in the real world. The normal explanation is that adverse policy shifts are prevented by the costs of damaging long-term contracts, reputation effects etc. As pointed out by Tirole (1989: 24–34), however, long-term relationships are subject to limitations due to outside opportunities.[2]

As will be seen, consideration of long-term contracts is not necessary to explain direct investment. MNEs operate across the boundaries of nation states, and are therefore in a position to play off potential host countries against each other. Doyle and van Wijnbergen (1984) and Eaton and Gersovitz (1983) represent two of the few theoretical studies that have considered host country competition in taxation. Instead of investigating the distribution of gains, which is the task of the present work, these studies assume perfect competition and zero profits net of tax.

It is evident that host country competition makes a difference to the distribution of the gains from direct investment. However, no previous studies have determined which taxes are established across countries. If a country taxes all the profit from an investment project, a firm has the option to set up a subsidiary in another country and produce there instead. But does this mean that countries must keep taxes low, or can all countries impose high taxes? To provide answers to such questions, in this chapter we determine the optimal taxation in a sequential bargaining framework.

Host countries are modelled as gaining from direct investment solely through corporate income tax. Of course, tax holidays are often regarded as worthwhile, although corporate income tax constitutes the most tangible host country gain. This implies that the net outcome of other effects is generally non-negative. Similarly, the fact that only temporary rather than permanent tax concessions are made implies that, on balance, other effects are negligible. This could be argued to justify our construction, and it is relatively straightforward to supplement the model with other effects entering as mere constants. Nevertheless, a comprehensive analysis of the welfare effects of direct investment requires a more detailed treatment of the functioning of subsidiaries, as well as host economies, than is attempted here.

The chapter is organized as follows. In the next section we present the set-up of the game, and in the following sections we investigate different model specifications. The case of two identical host countries when the irreversible cost required for direct investment only sustains production in the same period is considered first, and then we discuss the case in which the sunk cost sustains production in later periods as well. Next, countries are allowed to offer initial incentives. The possibility of dissimilar host countries is incorporated in the following section, the findings of which are robust with respect to any number of dissimilar countries. Finally the model results are compared and the conclusions are presented.

THE GAME

Consider a non-cooperative game with firms and countries which act as rational maximizers of their profits and socio-economic gains respectively. At any point in time, players maximize their gains given the best possible actions of other players in all time periods, which is consistent with the characterization of a Nash equilibrium. As pointed out by Johansen (1982), the Nash equilibrium is sometimes mistakenly interpreted as taking agents to be shortsighted concerning the behaviour of others. On the contrary, it requires a great deal of sophistication. Agents take all optimal responses, in any possible configurations, into consideration. In sequential bargaining, however, it is a weak solution concept since incredible threats are admitted. Any individually rational outcome can result in a Nash equilibrium. For this reason, we make use of the stronger concept of subgame perfect equilibrium defined by Selten (1975).

A combination of strategies constitutes a subgame perfect equilibrium if, in every subgame, the strategies relating to that subgame form a Nash equilibrium. In a subgame perfect equilibrium, an agent cannot be induced by another player's deviation from equilibrium to deviate himself. A plan remains optimal along an unanticipated path as well as along anticipated ones. The subgame perfect equilibrium is an improvement over Nash equilibrium in that incredible threats become less useful. In the following, the subgame perfect equilibrium will be referred to as 'equilibrium'.[3]

The object of study is a firm which, if it produces in a developing country, can generate a positive profit before tax. Many plausible constructions may motivate a positive profit. For simplicity, consider a firm which can produce and sell at home just one good at a price P, which is taken as given. Production can be located either at home or, through a subsidiary, in one of two possible host countries. The pre-tax profit R is

$$R = P - z - W_i \qquad i = H, C_1, C_2 \qquad (3.1)$$

where z is the cost of drawing on the parent's specific ownership advantage and w_i is the wage cost. H stands for the home country and C_1 and C_2 for the two potential host countries. The ownership advantage allows labour to be hired anywhere. Assume that

$$P = z + w_H > z + w_{C_1} = z + w_{C_2} \qquad (3.2)$$

i.e. C_1 and C_2 have the same wage level, which is strictly lower than w_H. If production takes place in H, we have $R = 0$; if it takes place in C_1 or C_2 it is assumed that $R = 1$. Thus, there is a potential real profit of one unit to be shared between the MNE and one of the host countries. This is then divided by the latter's tax rate ϕ.

Owing to their legislative power, countries are viewed as being able to negotiate ϕ at any time and discriminate policies between firms perfectly, which makes it possible to consider taxation of one firm at a time. Since firm-specific taxation seems the exception rather than the rule in the real world, this construction may at first seem disturbing. However, the factual tax is dependent on deductibility clauses, concessions given to local agents, performance requirements, local content rules, provision of investment incentives etc. Such policies are, indeed, generally levied on a case-by-case basis. Moreover, our construction is in line with the prevailing literature in the field, such as Doyle and van Wijnbergen (1984) and Shenfield (1984).

Focusing on the *ex ante–ex post* distinction, we view the life span of an investment project as represented by only one time period, meaning that a subsidiary depreciates completely after one period of production. The home country represents a zero profit alternative and is therefore not included in the game. This makes the set of players N consist of

$$N = \{F, C_1, C_2\} \tag{3.3}$$

where F is the investing firm. Since F can bargain with the two countries to obtain as low a level of tax as possible, the Walrasian 'market-clearing' tax would be zero (cf. Shaked and Sutton 1984) if it were not for two necessary qualifications. First, direct investment requires fixed and irreversible costs. Second, economic agents are not indifferent with respect to the actual timing of a gain.

Assume that the set-up of a subsidiary in C_1 or C_2 requires a fixed irreversible cost S added to the costs in (3.2). S is taken to be only a fraction of unity, so that there is still a potential profit to be made. Time is discrete, the time horizontal is infinite and the discount factor $\delta \in [0, 1]$. A good is sold in the same period as it is produced. Accordingly, revenues are obtained immediately. Although discounting needs no justification, one special interpretation in this context is that the MNE has partial market power, through a patent for example. The market can be saturated by one period's output but, if advantage is not taken of the opportunity, competitors gradually develop substitutes and reduce the good's real price as well as the potential profit.

Further assume that there are no budget constraints, meaning that direct investment can always be financed. However, we allow only one subsidiary to be set up in each period. The time unit therefore corresponds to the time needed for a firm to relocate its productive resources, so that the discount factor indicates how quickly the firm can relocate its productive resources. When $\delta = 1$ the host country can set up a subsidiary in the other country immediately. Together, S and δ characterize the 'mobility' of direct investment.

A host country is free to change ϕ at any time, and can be thought of as setting it *after* a subsidiary is established but before production takes place. Allowing ϕ to be set after production would lack economic sense since the whole life span of an investment project is represented by one time period. A tax might be revised subsequent to the spending of investment required to start up production, but cannot be collected after a project has depreciated. Since only one good is produced, the game ends when the decision to produce is made.

In the following sections, the game is set up and analysed in four different model specifications. Strategies and pay-off functions are presented case by case. It turns out that production always occurs in $t = 1$, when the potential gain of direct investment is largest, except when it is discouraged in the first place. However, the determination of an equilibrium requires a calculation of pay-offs in subsequent periods, which is in line with the established solution technique for a subgame perfect equilibrium. The model results are compared in a later section.

MODEL 1: NON-DEFERRABLE PRODUCTION

In this section, we assume that the irreversible cost S sustains production only in the same period. If the firm wishes to enter a country again, it will have to spend S anew. The options open to the players are

$$A_F^0 = \{in_{C_1}, in_{C_2}, e\} \qquad A_{FC_1} = \{q_1, in_{C_2}, e\},$$

$$A_{FC_2} = \{q_2, in_{C_1}, e\} \qquad A_{C_1} = A_{C_2} = [0, 1] \qquad (3.4)$$

where A_F^0 refers to the single-period action space of F in period zero, which is the state before any investment has been undertaken. A_{FC_1} is the action space of F when it has set up a subsidiary in C_1 and A_{FC_2} is the corresponding space when it has done so in C_2. The connotation in_{C_1} means setting up a subsidiary in C_1, e means exiting the game, i.e. not investing in any country, and q_1 means producing in C_1. A_{C_1} is the strategy space of C_1 and A_{C_2} that of C_2. Throughout, subscripts indicate agents and superscripts indicate time periods.

As can be seen, F makes only the discrete choices whether and where to invest and produce. If F chooses not to produce subsequent to investment, it withdraws to invest in the alternative country. There is always a possibility of ending the game, but after $t = 0$ that cannot represent the actual outcome since, if e dominates at any time, then it must prevent investment in the first place.[4] The countries set ϕ, which is a continuous variable taking a value between zero and unity. The game is symmetric with respect to the countries, which are identical *ex ante*. The choice of strategies is returned to below.

Figure 3.1 illustrates the game in extensive form. The pay-offs are denoted u_F, u_{C_1}, u_{C_2} or u_i, with $i = C_1, C_2$ when the countries' return is the same. In the first period $t = 0$, F has not invested in any country. Period $t = 1$, the first *ex post* stage, begins as F spends S (thought of as an instantaneous event) in either C_1 (in $_{C1}$) or C_2 (in $_{C2}$). This act, indicated by a solid rectangle, is followed by the host country setting ϕ^1. F then chooses production q^1 or withdrawal. Production means

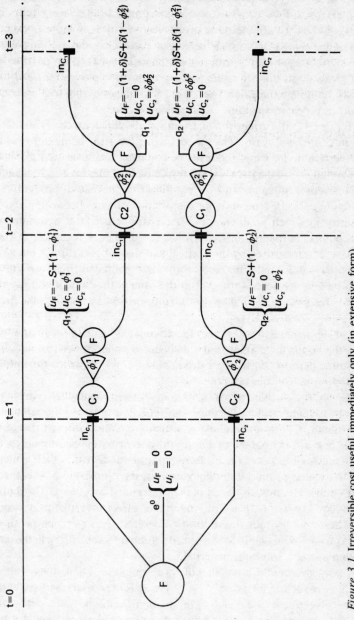

Figure 3.1 Irreversible cost useful immediately only (in extensive form)
Superscript = time   Subscript = agent $i = C_1 > C_2$ ■ = spent

that $R = 1$ is divided between the host country and the firm through ϕ^1. The country gains ϕ^1 and F gains $(1 - \phi^1) - S$. If F chooses not to produce, it invests in the other country instead. The game then continues in $t = 2$ with the same process as in $t = 1$ reiterated, the only difference being that costs and benefits are now discounted. F first spends S and, subsequent to an offered ϕ^2, chooses between production and withdrawal. In this way, the game can in principle be repeated endlessly, although the gain to be shared diminishes owing to discounting and the repeated spending of irreversible costs.[5]

Figure 3.2 illustrates the distribution of gains between F and C_1 or C_2 in coalitional form. The pay-off u_F of the firm is measured along the vertical axis, while those of the countries are measured along the horizontal axis to the right and left respectively of the origin. The diagonal t lines represent candidates for equilibria in the case of production in different periods, indicating the distribution of gains between F and the country in which production occurs. Extreme tax rates determine the end points. In diagrammatic terms, a larger ϕ corresponds to a lower outcome as measured by the vertical axis and a point further out along the horizontal axis. The erosion of the potential profit over time is reflected in the downward shift of the t lines. Investment is prevented in the first place if we end up beneath the horizontal axis, since the firm's pay-off is then negative.

To summarize, F maximizes the discounted value of profit after tax, and the countries maximize the discounted value of tax revenue. The outcome depends on whether production occurs, in which time period it occurs and on the tax rate.

Consider a situation in which F has invested in country 1. To maximize its tax revenue without at the same time discouraging the firm from producing, C_1 sets the highest ϕ_1^1 which guarantees F a return as high as its best alternative. Note that, in the one firm–one country case, F's only alternative is to exit, e^1. In relation to this C_1 can set $\phi_1^1 = 1$, i.e. tax the whole profit. With two countries, the possibility of investment in C_2 must be considered. ϕ_1^1 is then restrained by $(1 - \phi_1^1) \geq \delta (1 - \phi_2^2 - S)$.[6] In words, if a firm undertakes direct investment in a country, that country must leave the firm with at least as much profit net of tax as it would obtain from instead setting up a subsidiary in the other country in the subsequent period.

First, consider the possibility of Nash equilibria. Think of an arbitrary number a such that $0 \leq a \leq 1$. Say that F uses a strategy such that, given investment in a country, production occurs only if $\phi \leq a$. If $\phi > a$, F consequently withdraws without producing so that the host country earns zero. It is immediately clear that any ϕ can form a Nash

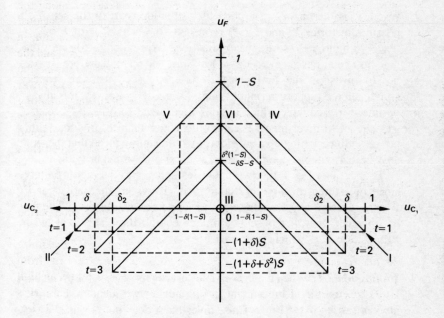

Figure 3.2 The distribution of gains (in coalitional form). Negative t slopes refer to U_F, U_{C_1}; positive t slopes refer to u_F, u_{C_2}

equilibrium. Whichever a is chosen by the firm, the host country maximizes its pay-off by offering $\phi = a$, since a higher tax prevents the country from obtaining any gain and a lower tax makes it earn less than what is attainable.

The failure to render a unique Nash equilibrium derives from the acceptance of incredible threats. This 'weakness' does not pertain to (subgame perfect) equilibria, which require that agents maximize pay-offs in all possible subgames. In a finite game, equilibrium can be identified by tracing optimal choices from the end backwards, i.e. from right to left in the extensive form. Since our gain is infinite, this method cannot be used. It is not difficult to construct one candidate for equilibrium, however. Consider the strategy combination $\hat{o}$

$$
\begin{aligned}
\hat{o}_{C_1} &= \phi_{C_i}(y^t) = 1 \ \forall \ y^t \ \epsilon \ Y \\
\hat{o}_F(y^0) &= e^0 \\
\hat{o}_F(y^t) &= q_{C_i} \ \forall \ \phi^t
\end{aligned} \tag{3.5}
$$

where y^t is the history of a particular situation, part of the set of all possible histories Y, and $\hat{o}_F(y^0)$ represents the behaviour of F in $t = 0$ according to the $\hat{o}$ strategy combination. Expression (3.5) states that both host countries always set $\phi = 1$ *ex post*, and that F therefore chooses not to invest in the first place. It is easily seen that the strategy combination $\hat{o}$ supports an equilibrium. Denote $\phi = 1 = \phi^*$. It is always optimal for a country which obtains investment to offer ϕ^* because, subsequent to investment, F cannot do better than to produce at this tax rate. Since setting up a subsidiary would simply mean that the sunk cost is lost without compensation, F choose e^0 to begin with.

The setting of ϕ in the two countries appears to interact infinitely, since investment in the other country is always an alternative for F. For this reason, any tax rate seems to support an equilibrium. The fact is, however, that $\hat{o}$ represents a unique equilibrium. This is stated in Proposition 3.1, which is proved below.

Proposition 3.1: When the irreversible cost cannot be used for production later, foreign direct investment in one out of two identical countries always results in $\phi^* = 1$. Thus, investment does not pay in the first place, so that e^0 is a unique equilibrium

Proof: Assume that investment has occurred in C_1 in $t = 1$. We know that ϕ can never exceed $\phi^* = 1$. Thus, any $\phi_1^{1**} \neq \phi_1^{1*}$ must be such that $\phi_1^{1**} < \phi_1^{1*}$. Assume that there exists a ϕ_1^{1**} such that $u_{C_1}(\phi_1^{1**}) > u_{C_1}(\phi_1^{1*})$. Since $\partial u_{C_1}/\partial \phi_1^1 > 0$, $u_{C_1}(\phi_1^{1**})$ must then stem from q_1^1 while $u_{C_1}(\phi_1^{1*})$ must stem from not q_1^1, because the inequality $u_{C_1}(\phi_1^{1**}) > u_{C_1}(\phi_1^{1*})$ cannot hold otherwise. C_2, presenting the only possible non-zero alternative for F, must set ϕ_2^2 so that $1 - \phi_1^{1*} < \delta(1 - \phi_2^2 - S) \leqslant 1 - \phi_1^{1**}$. But ϕ_2^2 would be set by C_2 as high as possible while compensating F for its best alternative rate of return. Thus, we will have $\delta(1 - \phi_2^2) = \delta^2(1 - \phi_1^3 - S)$. By using this equality, we would have that $1 - \phi_1^{1*} < \delta^2(1 - \phi_1^3 - S) - \delta S \leqslant 1 - \phi_1^{1**}$. But this is impossible, since the situation C_1 faces in $t = 3$ is exactly identical with that in $t = 1$. This must render $\phi_1^1 = \phi_1^3 = \phi^*$, ensuring that $\phi_2^2 = \phi^*$ is optimal for C_2. There is no viable strategy which can realize a better outcome for F than to produce at this tax rate. Since $\phi^1 = \phi^*$, F is bound to make a loss by investing in any country, ensuring that e^0 is a unique *ex ante* equilibrium.

We have seen that, while any tax can form a Nash equilibrium owing to a firm's ability to make incredible threats, there is a unique subgame perfect equilibrium. Once investment has been undertaken, it is always optimal for the chosen country to tax the whole profit from production. The outcome is represented in Figure 3.2 by point I for investment in C_1, and by point II for investment in C_2. Since either results in a negative *ex ante* pay-off for the firm ($- S$), III is the unique *ex ante* equilibrium. As in the one firm–one country case, direct investment is prevented in the first place because host countries cannot commit future behaviour. The novelty is that the interaction between two alternative host countries, in setting their optimal taxes, prevents them from competing effectively. No collusion is involved, but a host country is still known always to set $\phi = 1$ *ex post* the undertaking of direct investment, making a firm's threat to withdraw incredible.

The one firm–one country result is thereby seen to hold under these circumstances. This may seem of little practical relevance since direct investment does occur in the real world. However, the implication may be, for example, that agents are irrational, information is incomplete, violation of contracts results in indirect costs such as those of damaging a business relationship that involves a sequence of projects, host countries offer initial incentives to firms or that more than two host countries compete for gains. The latter two possibilities are examined later. Before that, we consider the result's robustness with respect to the specification of technology.

MODEL 2: PRODUCTION AT ANY TIME

The set-up here is identical with that in the preceding section except for the nature of the fixed irreversible cost of setting up a subsidiary. We now assume that a subsidiary can be used for production in any future time period. The game is shown in extensive form in Figure 3.3, while we refer back to Figure 3.2 for an illustration of the outcome in the coalitional form.

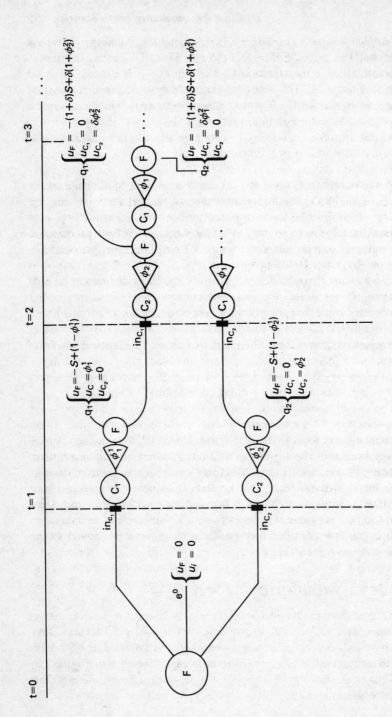

Figure 3.3 Irreversible cost useful in production at any time (in extensive form)

In $t = 0$ and $t = 1$, the game is the same as in the preceding section. If the MNE does not produce in the first period, however, it can set up a subsidiary in the other country as well in $t = 2$ and still produce in the first country, i.e. F can postpone the decision whether to produce in a country without losing S. In other words, F is able to diversify its production apparatus internationally.

Again, countries can bargain with a firm for a changed tax rate at any time. Bargaining is frictionless so that any number of offers can be exchanged within a time period. If a subsidiary is set up in both countries, the two have to compete with each other to secure any gain. In this case, the Walrasian market clearing ϕ_1^2 is clearly zero.[7] Given that $\delta \geqslant (1 + \delta)S$, i.e. the value of production in $t = 2$ surpasses the cost of spending S in $t = 1$ and $t = 2$, F can consequently realize this outcome in $t = 2$ and gain the whole profit net of setting up two subsidiaries. This is marked point VI in Figure 3.2.

Assume that C_1 obtains a project in the first period. In order to gain anything, C_1 must set ϕ_1^1 subject to the constraint $1 - \phi_1^1 \geqslant \delta(1 - S)$. This means compensating F for its best alternative rate of return in $t = 2$. As $\partial u_1 / \partial \phi_1 > 0$, the solution is $\phi_1^{1*} = 1 - \delta(1 - S)$, which is the highest tax for which the constraint holds. The resulting distribution is

$$
\begin{aligned}
u_F &= \delta(1 - S) - S \\
u_{C_1} &= 1 - \delta(1 - S) \\
u_{C_2} &= 0
\end{aligned}
\tag{3.6}
$$

The host country can only tax as much as the value of production before tax would diminish by having it deferred to the next period in the other country. This means that the MNE obtains an amount corresponding to the entire profit in $t = 2$, less the cost of setting up two subsidiaries. The firm is indifferent *ex ante* between the two countries, since both would set ϕ^{1*} subsequent to investment. The outcome of direct investment in the two countries is represented by points IV and V respectively in Figure 3.2. Either is a unique equilibrium given investment in a country. By analogy with the preceding section, no threat of deviation is credible. Any $\phi^{1**} \neq \phi^{1*}$ must be inferior for a country since a lower tax means less tax revenue and a higher tax makes F invest in the other country as well.

In contrast with model 1, we have in this case demonstrated that effective host country competition restricts the level of taxation. Provided that there is a net benefit from production in the second period, direct investment pays and is undertaken in the first period. The distribution of gains favours the MNE, the smaller the irreversible cost and the larger the discount factor. Discounting diminishes the firm's share because the alternative investment opportunity is weakened. With $\delta = 1$, we have $u_F = 1 - 2S$ as the best possible outcome for an MNE in this model set-up.

Thus, the outcome obtained in the previous section – no direct investment in equilibrium – does not apply when subsidiaries can be set up in both countries before the decision where to produce needs to be taken. Indeed, it appears plausible that irreversible costs can support production later. However, as will be seen in the following, the nature of the irreversible costs is unimportant when initial incentives are allowed.

MODEL 3: INVESTMENT INCENTIVES OFFERED BY TWO IDENTICAL COUNTRIES

So far the firm has made the first move. However, the countries have had a potential for real gains if selected as host. They can therefore be expected to make efforts *ex ante* to obtain investment, which can frequently be observed as subsidized infrastructure or tax holidays. One view of tax holidays is that a country uses them to signal its nature when there is asymmetric information about its productivity (Bond and Samuelson 1986). However, this does not explain the strategic interaction between alternative host countries, which indeed seems an important factor behind the increase in investment incentives that has taken place in the last decades.

Using a sequential bargaining model in which alternative host countries compete for gains from direct investment, Doyle and van Wijnbergen (1984) explained tax holidays as a compensation for the 'lock-in' effects of sunk costs in a country. They found that a host country always offers a tax holiday whose discounted value compensates exactly for the irreversible cost required for direct investment. Nevertheless, the distribution of gains is not really considered. Underlying their result is the assumption that perfect competition between firms achieves a zero *ex ante* return net of tax. Moreover, their model does not explain how the incentives are affected by the properties of countries and, in particular, the degree of competition that prevails between them. These matters will be addressed here.

In the following, the strategy space of F is unchanged, but those of the countries are extended by an investment incentive k. This is a continuous variable that takes a positive number. The game is presented in extensive form in Figure 3.4. The sunk cost only supports production in the same period but, as will be seen, this is no longer of importance.[8] Only the path when investment is undertaken in

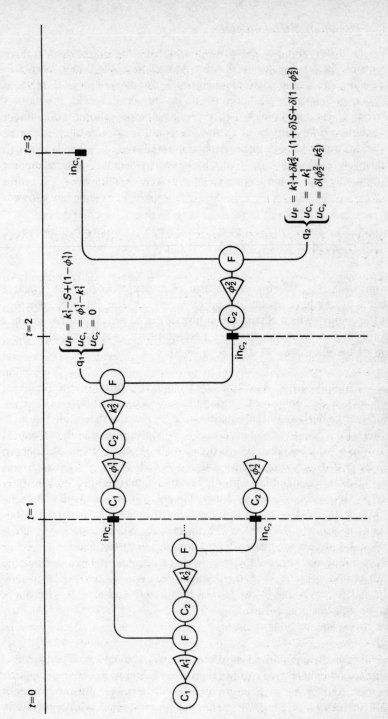

Figure 3.4 Initial incentives offered by two identical countries (in extensive form)

$$u_F = k_1^1 - S + (1 - \phi_1^1)$$
$$u_{C_1} = \phi_1^1 - k_1^1$$
$$u_{C_2} = 0$$

$$u_F = k_1^1 + \delta k_2^2 - (1 + \delta)S + \delta(1 - \phi_2^2)$$
$$u_{C_1} = -k_1^1$$
$$u_{C_2} = \delta(\phi_2^2 - k_2^2)$$

C_1 first is shown, since the game is symmetrical with respect to the countries. Beginning in $t = 0$, the countries have the option to offer k^1. Again, bidding is frictionless so that F can reject many offers and still accept one in $t = 0$. Accepting an *ex ante* offer, say k_1^1, F obtains k_1^1 from C_1 as $t = 1$ begins. Since k is a compensation for S, these payments can be thought of as simultaneous. C_1 then sets ϕ_1^1. Before F has to decide how to respond, k_2^2 is offered by C_2. Either F rejects k_2^2 in preference to q_1^1, or it accepts k_2^2 and invests in C_2, spending S as k_2^2 is received at the beginning of $t = 2$. C_2 then sets ϕ_2^2.

As the two countries are symmetrical, a country can obtain investment in $t = 1$ only if it offers a k at least as large as that of the other country. A certain k is offered only if it pays. Again there is a unique equilibrium, which is stated as proposition 3.2. It is proved below.

Proposition 3.2: When two identical countries can offer investment incentives, we have in equilibrium $k_j^{1*} = \phi_j^{1*} = 1 - \delta(1 - S)$, where j is the country which obtains direct investment. It is inconclusive which country is chosen, so that there are two equilibria. In either the distribution of the gain is $u_F = 1 - S$, $u_j = 0$.

Proof: Assume that k_1^1 is accepted by F. q_1^1 then requires $1 - \phi_1^1 \geqslant \delta(k_2^2 - S + 1 - \phi_2^2)$. In order to attract the subsidiary, C_2 offers $k_2^2 \leqslant \phi^2$. This can be written as an equality since C_2 will exhaust all but an infinitesimal gain to attract investment. By shifting location F can earn $\delta(1 - S)$, which makes ϕ_1^1 restricted by $1 - \phi_1^1 \geqslant \delta(1 - S)$. Since $\partial u_1/\partial\theta_1 > 0$, C_1 maximizes u_1 through $\phi_1^{1*} = 1 - \delta(1 - S)$, which is the highest tax compatible with q_1^1. The two countries are identical, so that ϕ^{1*} would be offered by either. Competition makes both offer $k^1 = k^{1*} = 1 - \delta(1 - S)$ *ex ante*, making it indeterminate which one obtains investment. No $k^{1**} \neq k^{1*}$ can make a country better off, since $k^{1**} < k^{1*}$ makes the other country obtain investment and $k^{1**} > k^{1*}$ incurs a real loss since $\phi^{1*} < k^{1**}$ in that case. Any $\phi^{1**} \neq \phi^{1*}$ must similarly be inferior. $\phi^{1**} < \phi^{1*}$ means less tax revenue and $\phi^{1**} > \phi^{1*}$ makes F relocate to the other country. k^{1*} and ϕ^{1*} thus form a unique equilibrium, ensuring $u_F = k^{1*} - S + (1 - \phi^{1*}) = 1 - S$, and zero gain for both countries.

Note that the equilibrium tax is the same as in model 2, and that again there are two alternative equilibria corresponding to direct investment in either country in $t = 1$. However, the whole net profit from investment accrues to the MNE. The distribution of gains is represented by point VI in Figure 3.2, irrespective of which country is chosen as host. In this case, the opportunity to compete with initial incentives prevents countries from capturing any gain from direct investment.

By assuming that a firm is deprived of all profit, Doyle and van Wijnbergen (1984) concluded that the irreversible cost is shifted onto the host country by means of a tax holiday. In contrast, we have shown that host country competition shifts the whole surplus from production (net of the irreversible cost) to the firm. Competition between countries forces them to offer the largest k that they can afford. The discounted value S of the tax holiday obtained by Doyle and van Vijnbergen applies to k^{1*} (as well as ϕ^{1*}) only when $\delta = 1$. If $\delta < 1$, k^{1*} and ϕ^{1*} are larger. The discount factor determines the size of the investment incentive, but leaves the equilibrium distribution of the gains unaffected.

So far we have considered only identical host countries. In practice, investment opportunities are likely to be different in different countries owing to capital market imperfections, inequalities in labour productivity, geographical location etc. This possibility is incorporated in the model presented in the next section.

MODEL 4: INVESTMENT INCENTIVES OFFERED BY DISSIMILAR COUNTRIES

The preceding models are of limited relevance for the inter-country pattern of investment since only identical countries have been considered. The distribution of the gain has concerned a firm and a randomly selected host country. In practice, it is unlikely that the pre-tax profit generated from direct investment in two countries would be exactly the same. Moreover, a profit could probably be made in more than two countries, which opens up the possibility of competition between many potential host countries. As will be seen, the results obtained are robust with respect to any number of dissimilar countries.

Assume that the pre-tax profit *ex post* is 1 in C_1, as before, but 1 $- \beta$ in C_2, where $\beta \in [0, 1]$. The larger β is, the larger is the difference in pre-tax profit between the two countries. Consequently, C_1 is the best location in terms of overall resource allocation, and C_2 is the second best. With initial incentives admitted, model 3 can be thought of as applicable when $\beta = 0$. Then assume that $\beta > 0$, but that there is effective host country competition, i.e. $\beta \leqslant 1 - S - \delta S$. See Figure 3.5 for the extensive form. From the preceding section, we know that C_1 offers approximately $k_1^2 = \phi_1^2$ if the subsidiary is first set up in

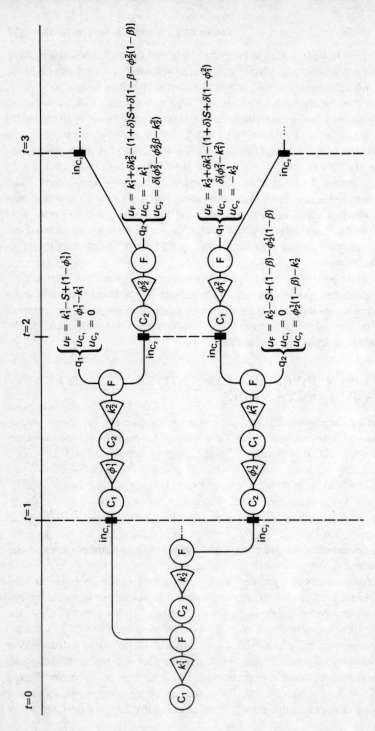

Figure 3.5 Initial incentives offered by two dissimilar countries (in extensive form)

C_2. In the same way, C_2 can offer $k_2^2 \leqslant (1 - \beta)\phi_2^2$ if the subsidiary is first set up in C_1. Thus, if in_{C_1} has occurred in $t = 1$, C_1 sets its tax restricted by $1 - \phi_1^1 \geqslant \delta(1 - \beta - S)$. In the corresponding position, C_2 is restricted by $(1 - \phi_2^1)(1 - \beta) \geqslant \delta(1 - S)$. For each respective country, utility maximization ensures that $\phi_1^1 = 1 - \delta(1 - \beta - S)$ and $\phi_2^1 = 1 - \delta(1 - S)/(1 - \beta)$.

For C_1, ϕ_1^1 represents the *ex post* profit. For C_2, the *ex post* profit is $\phi_2^1(1 - \beta) = 1 - \beta - \delta(1 - S)$. The *ex post* profit is always larger in C_1 than in C_2, the difference being $(1 + \delta)\beta$, meaning that C_1 can afford the largest k^1. Note that $\phi_1^1 > 0$, while $\phi_2^1(1 - \beta)$ may or may not be. But a country will not, of course, offer any incentive *ex ante* if it cannot expect to reap any profit *ex post*. Depending on whether C_2 can offer $k_2^1 > 0$ or not, $k_1^{1*} = \max [1 - \beta - \delta(1 - S), 0]$, or rather infinitesimally more (being the smallest k_1^1 which guarantees in_{C_1}). *Ex post*, C_1 ensures production through $\phi_1^{1*} = 1 - \delta(1 - \beta - S)$, since this exactly compensates F for its best alternative investment. Analogous with the earlier sections, it can be verified that no $k_1^{1**} \neq k_1^{1*}$ or $\phi_1^{1**} \neq \phi_1^{1*}$ can pay. Investment and production in C_1 under k_1^{1*} and ϕ_1^{1*} represent a unique equilibrium.

Let us refer to $k_1^1 > 0$ as case 1, and $k_1^1 \approx 0$ as case 2. Case 1 is applicable when there is a fairly small difference between the two countries and/or substantial discounting. It is restricted by $\beta < 1 - \delta(1 - S)$, or $\delta < (1 - \beta)/(1 - S)$. If these are not fulfilled, we have case 2. The distribution in the two cases is (cf. Table 3.1).[9]

$$u_F = k_1^{1*} - S + (1 - \phi_1^{1*}) \quad \approx \quad \begin{cases} 1 - S - (1 + \delta)\beta & \text{in case 1} \\ \delta(1 - \beta - S) - S & \text{in case 2} \end{cases}$$

$$\text{(3.7)}$$

$$u_{C_1} = - k_1^{1*} + \phi_1^{1*} \quad \approx \quad \begin{cases} (1 + \delta)\beta & \text{in case 1} \\ 1 - \delta(1 - \beta - S) & \text{in case 2} \end{cases}$$

$$u_{C_2} = 0 \quad \text{in cases 1 and 2}$$

As can be seen, the equilibrium distribution depends on the parameters β, S and δ. The role of β, which indicates the competitive strength of the best host country relative to the second best, is straightforward. The larger β is, the larger is the host country's share of the gains. This result is stated as proposition 3.3.

Proposition 3.3: A firm is better off the more even the profit distribution between two alternative host countries, while a country is better off the more superior its investment opportunities to those of the second best country.

Figure 3.6 illustrates the distribution of gains for varying β, δ and S

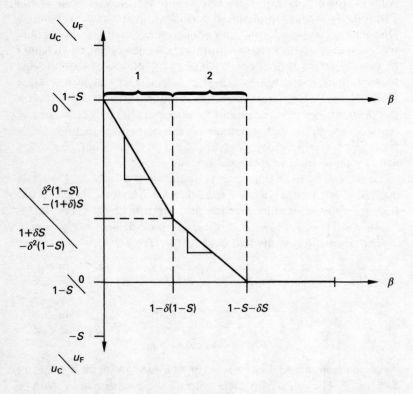

Figure 3.6 Equilibrium distribution at different values of ß

held constant. u_F is measured up the vertical axis, and u_C is measured down the axis. The negative slope indicates that the host country's share increases in ß. When ß = 0 we have, as stated in Proposition 3.2, u_F = 1 − S and u_C = 0. As noted, we then have the special case analysed in model 3. It should be borne in mind that it is then indeterminate which country obtains investment and that neither of them will gain anything from attracting it. As soon as β surpasses zero by an infinitesimal amount, it is immediately given that the best country can outbid the second best, and that this country is able to capture part of the profit. The results hold for any number of potential host countries, since C_1 and C_2 are merely the best and second best countries in terms of pre-tax profit. C_1 may offer the largest initial incentive *ex ante* and C_2 is willing to exhaust all its gain to attract direct investment.

As long as we are in case 1, S does not affect the distribution, while a smaller δ favours F and diminishes the country's share. The role of δ contrasts with model 2 and may appear counter-intuitive. Discounting favours F since it weakens the alternative host country's competitiveness and therefore enables the second best country to offer a larger k_2^1 to begin with, forcing the best to offer more as well. As can be seen in Figure 3.7, a smaller δ means a larger intercept for k, i.e. k's value at $\beta = 0$. This dominates the reverse effect on ϕ^1.

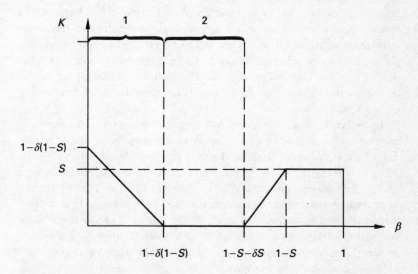

Figure 3.7 Equilibrium relation between k and β

In case 2, on the other hand, the situation is similar to model 2. Here, the outcome is less favourable to F, the larger S is and the smaller δ is. In this case k^1 is approximately zero in any case, while a smaller δ weakens the competitiveness of the alternative country and raises the equilibrium tax rate. This holds as long as $\beta \leqslant 1 - S - \delta S$. When β lies in the interval $1 - S - \delta S < \Omega < \beta\ 1 - S$, the host country competition is so weak *ex post* that the profit net of tax in C_1 is sufficient to cover only part of the sunk cost. Since this is known to F, C_1 must offer an initial incentive *ex ante* to compensate for the loss. Finally, when $\beta \geqslant 1 - S$, there is no effective host country competition at all *ex post*. We are back in the one firm–one country case and F must be offered an initial incentive which compensates for the whole irreversible cost.

Thus, an initial incentive is paid if there is either very weak or very fierce host country competition. In the latter case the incentive is greater, and the host country's share of the gain smaller, the fiercer the competition (see Figure 3.7).

COMPARISON OF THE MODEL RESULTS

The equilibrium distribution of profits between an MNE and the chosen host country is summarized in Table 3.1 for each of the models presented above. If production occurs, it is always in the first time period when the total gain is the largest possible $(1 - S)$. The total pay-off is the sum of the *ex ante* and *ex post* components. *Ex ante* refers to payments made when a subsidiary is set up, and *ex post* refers to payments associated with production. The distribution of gains is also specified for the case when subsidiaries can be set up in the other country without delay, i.e. the case when $\delta = 1$. The column $1/(\partial u/\partial \delta)$ shows by a positive or negative sign which part is favoured by more discounting of the future.

In model 1, when there are two identical potential host countries, the irreversible cost can only support production in the same period, no initial incentives are allowed and a country which obtains investment would tax the entire profit. Thus, direct investment is prevented in the first place. This result is overturned in model 2, where the irreversible cost can sustain production in future periods. In this case, a host country taxes only as much as the value of production before tax would diminish by deferring it to the other country in the next period. The opportunity for an MNE to diversify its production apparatus internationally limits a host country's ability to tax a subsidiary. Direct investment is undertaken provided that the pre-tax

Table 3.1 Summary of equilibrium properties

Model 1: Irreversible cost useful immediately only, no initial incentive
  Period of production: –

Model 2: Irreversible cost useful later, no initial incentive
  Condition for equilibrium as below: $\delta \geqslant S + \delta S$ (otherwise, no investment)

Distribution of gains

Part	Ex ante	Ex post	Total	Outcome if $\delta = 1$	$1/(\partial u/\partial \delta)$
u_F	$- S$	$\delta(1 - S)$	$\delta(1 - S) - S$	$1 - 2S$	–
u_C	0	$1 - \delta(1 - S)$	$1 - \delta(1 - S)$	S	+

Period of production: 1

Model 3: Initial incentives allowed, identical countries

Distribution of gains

Part	Ex ante	Ex post	Total	Outcome if $\delta = 1$	$1/(\partial u/\partial \delta)$
u_F	$1 - \delta(1 - S) - S$	$\delta(1 - S)$	$1 - S$	$1 - S$	0
u_C	$-[1 - \delta(1 - S)]$	$1 - \delta(1 - S)$	0	0	0

Period of production: 1

Model 4: Initial incentives allowed dissimilar countries

Case 1. Conditions for equilibrium as below: $\delta < (1 - \beta)/(1 - S)$, equivalent to $\beta < 1 - \delta(1 - S)$ (otherwise, see case 2)
  If $\beta = 0$, model 3 is applicable

Distribution of gains

Part	Ex ante	Ex post	Total	Outcome if $\delta = 1$	$1/(\partial u/\partial \delta)$
u_F	$1 - \beta - \delta(1 - S) - S$	$\delta(1 - \beta - S)$	$1 - S - (1 + \delta)\beta$	$1 - S - 2\beta$	+
u_C	$-[1 - \beta - \delta(1 - S)]$	$1\,\delta(1 - \beta - S)$	$(1 + \delta)\beta$	2β	–

Period of production: 1

Case 2. Conditions for equilibrium as below: $\delta \geqslant (1 - \beta)/1 - S)$, equivalent to $\beta \geqslant 1 - \delta(1 - S)$ (otherwise, see case 1) and $\beta \leqslant 1 - S - \delta S$

  Approximate distribution of gains

Part	Ex ante	Ex post	Total	Outcome if $\delta = 1$	$1/(\partial u/\partial \delta)$
u_F	$- S$	$\delta(1 - \beta - S)$	$\delta(1 - \beta - S) - S$	$1 - \beta - 2S$	–
u_C	0	$1 - \delta(1 - \beta - S)$	$1 - \delta(1 - \beta - S)$	$\beta + S$	+

Period of production: 1

Notes: F, firm; C, country obtaining direct investment.

profit is sufficient to finance the establishment of two subsidiaries. The gain of the investing firm diminishes with discounting and the size of the sunk cost, since these factors weaken the alternative of producing in the other country.

The results of the first two models hinge on the limiting assumption that initial incentives are not allowed. When they are, as in models 3 and 4, the nature of the irreversible cost is unimportant. In model 3, where there are two identical countries, the whole profit net of the irreversible cost accrues to the MNE. The host countries' ability to compete for direct investment by offering initial incentives deprives them of any gains. The most general results derive from model 4, where host countries are allowed to be dissimilar in the quality of their investment opportunities.

As soon as the two countries are at all different, there is again room for host country earnings. The country with the most favourable investment opportunities obtains a project, meaning that the pattern of direct investment is undistorted by effective host country competition. The host country earns more, the more superior its investment opportunities are relative to those of the second best country. The distribution of gains is also influenced by the 'mobility' of investment in the form of the discount factor and the sunk cost. The outcome will accord with case 1 if there is sufficient discounting or a sufficiently small difference between the two countries. Otherwise it will accord with case 2. The two specifications differ in that the second best country can afford to offer an initial incentive in the former, but not in the latter. The initial incentive is larger, the fiercer the host country competition, but it may also be paid when there is very weak competition.

CONCLUDING REMARKS

In the one firm–one country case with complete information, it is well known that optimal host country taxation prevents direct investment in the first place. *Ex post* the establishment of a subsidiary, the host country is able to tax the whole profit so that the investing MNE loses its sunk cost. The inability of the host country to commit its future behaviour results in a suboptimal outcome as a potential mutual profit for a firm and a host country is forgone. This kind of underinvestment is also known as the Williamson problem of *ex post* opportunism. The fact that a good deal of direct investment is still undertaken in the real world is often explained by the costs of damaging long-term contracts, reputation effects etc. However, empirical studies have had difficulties in demonstrating such costs.

In this chapter we have analysed taxation given that potential host countries compete for gains from direct investment. Such competition between host countries has been verified empirically by Guisinger (1985). The analysis can be viewed as a demonstration of the importance of outside opportunities in bargaining. Previous studies, such as those by Eaton and Gersovitz (1983) and Doyle and van Wijnbergen (1984), have studied the outcome of host country competition given perfect competition and zero profits. No earlier work has determined the actual division of profits through taxation when there are competing countries. Using a sequential bargaining game, we have analysed the taxes that would prevail in a subgame perfect equilibrium in which host countries can discriminate their behaviour between firms. The pragmatic determination of taxes on a case by case basis can be seen from the widespread use of deductibility clauses, concessions given to local agents, investment incentives etc.

The major outcome of the analysis is that taxation by effectively competing host countries leads to direct investments being undertaken in the country with the most favourable investment opportunities. The gain of the host country depends on the superiority of its investment opportunities in relation to those of the second best country, and the mobility of an investment project. Direct investment is prevented only in the implausible case where there are two exactly identical host countries, the sunk cost is able solely to sustain immediate production and no initial incentives are allowed.

The result obtained by Doyle and van Wijnbergen (1984), that a host country offers an initial incentive which corresponds exactly to the sunk cost, is found to hold only when countries are identical and the discount factor is unity, or when there is no effective host country competition. When countries are dissimilar but compete effectively, an initial incentive may or may not be needed for investment to be undertaken. Its value depends on the degree of dissimilarity and the discount factor, except for the sunk cost.

It should be made clear that this chapter merely represents a point of departure for a more realistic analysis. In practice, adjustments will be required in order to study specific investment projects and countries. Moreover, 'taxation' has referred to the range of *ex post* policy measures that manipulate the behaviour of MNEs. As discussed in Chapter 2, not all such policies aim at foreign exchange earnings. In particular, direct investment is likely to result in external effects, such as a spread of technology to domestic firms or environmental effects. The role of host country competition has been particularly debated in relation to the latter. In order to examine to what extent the results obtained here are also applicable when there are external economies, the next chapter extends the analysis to host country competition for pollution intensive direct investment. Thereafter, we turn to the other major host country policy – nationalization.

4   Foreign exchange versus pollution

INTRODUCTION

Like any economic activity, direct investment usually results not only in profits, but also in various external economies. It is well known that the pursuit of private gain does not maximize social welfare when there are external economies – meaning that market-priced transactions do not incorporate all the costs and benefits associated with transactions between economic agents. One category of external economies, which has increasingly attracted attention as important for the undertaking of direct investment, is 'environmental' effects (see, for example, James 1981). Activities which result in costly environmental effects, unless checked by pollution abatement, are referred to as 'pollution intensive' in the following.

As made clear, direct investment is motivated by the expectation that the transactions internalized abroad will generate a net benefit. Likewise, direct investment in pollution intensive activities may be motivated by the lack of an internalization of the costs of pollution. An increasing concern with environmental effects in industrialized countries during recent decades has materialized in higher operation costs. Walter (1972) was the first to prophesy that this would result in extensive pollution intensive direct investment in developing countries, where regulations remain less strict.

A relatively high assimilative capacity for pollutants in a country, or a low appreciation of environmental quality, constitutes an advantage which can be expected to be exploited. MNEs, which operate across the boundaries of nation states, are well suited to locate production where it is the most efficient. Owing to their ability to play individual countries against each other, however, it has been argued that MNEs 'blackmail' individual countries to accept environmental degradation as a price for obtaining investment projects. This would cause too much pollution and possibly distort the pattern of direct investment.

To investigate these matters, we apply the framework developed in Chapter 3 to host country competition for pollution intensive direct investment. The term taxation (as used elsewhere in the study) is split up into 'taxation' and 'environmental protection'. The former is thought of as concerned with foreign exchange earnings, and the latter with reduction of pollution. In fact, environmental protection is seldom subject to universal standards, but a great deal comes about via explicit or implicit negotiation between MNEs and national governments, not least in developing countries (cf. UNCTC 1985b). Whether it is designed as regulation, tax incentives, subsidies or a market for emission rights is not considered here. Our concern is the level of protection chosen.

In this chapter we demonstrate how the findings of Chapter 3 can help to illuminate the role of host country taxation for a specific category of investment. The question is also to what extent the results obtained in that chapter are in any fundamental sense affected by the inclusion of external economies, here in the form of an adverse impact on the host country's environment. To clarify some deviations from observations in the real world, we discuss the importance of imperfections in capital markets, information and 'government failure'. One aspect of environmental effects which is not considered is their possible crossing of national boundaries. We are limited to effects which are internal to the nation states in which pollution occurs.[1]

The outline of the chapter is as follows. We first present the background by surveying the importance of MNEs in pollution intensive industries in developing countries. Building on the analysis in Chapter 3, we then analyse host country competition for pollution intensive direct investment. The implications for the pattern of direct investment are clarified in the following section. Imperfections in our model are considered in the penultimate section and finally we summarize the chapter.

POLLUTION INTENSIVE ACTIVITIES AND DIRECT INVESTMENT

Environmental problems may arise as a consequence of almost any economic activity. The following sources of environmental effects were discussed by Walter (1975): gaseous discharges, liquid and solid discharges, thermal discharges, noise, radiation, disposal of solid waste, degradation of natural scenery and terrain, including the elimination of recreational opportunities, endangering of wildlife species and congestion. Broadly speaking, we can distinguish between two kinds of pollution: production and consumption pollution.[2] We are concerned only with the former kind. An incorporation of consumption pollution would require consideration of the disposal of goods which have been forbidden or rejected in industrialized countries. However, the two are often intertwined, with the latter enforcing the former.

We may ask whether the environmental impact of direct investment deserves any special attention. At least two arguments, apart from the MNEs' possible capacity to blackmail individual countries, have been brought forward to explain why there might be such a need. First, the pure scope of these firms in pollution intensive industries makes their environmental record matter. Second, their dominance in technology gives them a general influence on industrial processes. In this section we discuss to what extent these two arguments motivate any special concern with the environmental impact of direct investment. In the subsequent sections we address the matter of bargaining between MNEs and potential host countries which compete for gains from direct investment.

UNCTC (1985b) suggested operational definitions for pollution intensive activities based on the environmental policy attention attracted, environmental control data and relative operating costs for cleaning. The sectors on these grounds identified as pollution intensive were largely chemicals, the agro-industry, aluminium, iron and steel, motor vehicles, non-ferrous metals, petroleum and coal products, pulp and paper, and stone, clay and glass products. The sum of direct and indirect costs of environmental controls have been estimated to average some 39–52 per cent of the total costs in some of these industries.[3]

How important are MNEs in pollution intensive industries in developing countries? There are only tentative answers. The developing countries expanded their shares of the world's industrial value added in such industries between 1973 and 1980. Nevertheless, as of 1980, they had an overall share of value added greater than 25 per cent in just two branches – tobacco and petroleum refineries. The industrial expansion was in many cases achieved mainly by domestic industry, but Dunning and Pearce (1981) demonstrated considerable direct investment in practically all the pollution intensive industries. The lending industry group for direct investment is chemicals, including intermediate and final consumer goods such as petrochemicals, pharmaceuticals, paints, plastic products, fertilizers and pesticides. Mining, petroleum extraction and refining, agri-business, refining of heavy metals, wood and paper processing and motor vehicles also rank among the most important.

Investment data from individual home countries as well as host countries further verify that there is considerable direct investment in pollution intensive industries in developing countries. However, the consequences must be evaluated with respect to whether direct investment substitutes for domestic production or adds net to it. Although there seem to be plenty of examples of both kinds, this is generally difficult to know, and will depend on the time range considered.

The sheer size of direct investment alone does not allow us to determine its importance. The crucial question is how the MNEs' technology compares with that of domestic firms, and how the latter are influenced. MNEs play a first-hand role in the inter-country diffusion of technology in general, and in environmental management technology in particular. The transfers may be embodied in new investment, training, trade letters, licensing of control processes, direct sales of products or services etc. The availability of advanced environmental management must, of course, be separated from its application. Advanced pollution control is in general not desired by affiliates, and is seldom forced upon them by parents. While the technologies employed by affiliates in developing countries tend to be more polluting than those at home, there is systematic evidence that they are less so than corresponding domestic firms (UNCTC 1985b). However, there are considerable differences between individual MNEs.[4]

Given the scope of MNEs in pollution intensive industries and their importance for technology transfers, it must be concluded that their environmental impact on developing countries, whether good or bad, direct or indirect, is an issue of great concern. However, given large differences in environmental protection between industrialized and developing countries, pollution intensive industries can sooner or later be expected to flourish in the latter under any circumstances. Since MNEs normally employ a less polluting technology than domestic firms, direct investment *per se* is not crucial for possible environmental problems. Shedding light on pollution in developing countries calls rather for studies of pollution intensive activities in general. Thus, we are left with the bargaining strength of MNEs as an argument for why they would require special attention in this context. In the following, we add negative external economies on the environment to the model framework presented in Chapter 3.

BARGAINING WITH ENVIRONMENTAL PROTECTION

Pearson and Pryor (1978) argued that requirements of pollution abatement should neither favour nor discriminate against foreign as opposed to domestic firms. Throughout, the required level of cleaning should reflect the real resource costs in relation to the benefits of the social damage avoided. The crucial question here is whether host countries which compete for gains from direct investment have an incentive to deviate from the level of pollution control where the marginal cost equals the marginal social benefit.

Let us briefly review the case when MNEs and dissimilar host countries compete for profits and socio-economic gains respectively. MNEs choose the country in which to invest, and countries discriminate their policies *vis-à-vis* MNEs perfectly. Under these circumstances, we have seen that there is a unique subgame perfect equilibrium in which production occurs in the country with the most favourable investment opportunities. The tax rate is determined by the returns to a project in the best country relative to the second best, and the project's 'mobility' as given by the sunk cost and the discount factor. The reason is that a host country, *ex post* the set-up of a subsidiary, has to compensate an MNE for what it would earn from moving to another country and producing there instead. In order to gain anything, that second best country is prepared to exhaust practically all its gains to attract the project.

In equilibrium, a country which represents strictly better investment opportunities than its competitors has to give up only part of its gains, and is still able to attract direct investment. The smaller the difference from the second best country, the less of the gain the first best country is able to capture. Countries which represent the second or third best opportunities stretch their offers until they exhaust all their potential gains, but they are still unable to obtain a project since the best country taxes production just short of making it pay for the MNE to move.

This framework can be applied to pollution intensive direct investment which, in addition to profits, causes negative external effects. For the projects in question, countries can bargain not only with tax cuts, subsidies and incentives, but also with lax environmental protection. How much a host country has to give up to obtain direct investment still depends on the competitive strength of its investment opportunities in relation to those of competing countries, and on the mobility of investment. However, a country must now decide what combination of tax earnings and pollution control it desires. The choice is essentially between obtaining foreign exchange and preventing environmental degradation.

In terms, of the goods–bads box in Figure 2.1 (p. 31), the outcome of MNE–host country bargaining is along a diagonal line indicating the opportunity cost of the MNE, determined in turn by the attractiveness of the best alternative host country. What a host country gives up to obtain a project depends on its relative evaluation of foreign exchange and environmental quality. At the margin of how much a host country can acquire from an MNE, and yet retain a project, it has to balance one more dollar in pollution abatement against a dollar less of foreign exchange. Meanwhile, the benefit of pollution abatement is given by the social value of environmental protection. The social benefit of cleaning should equal the cost of pollution abatement at the margin, which should equal the social scarcity value of foreign exchange. There is nothing in this situation which motivates an environmental protection which deviates from the socially optimal level. Effective host country competition does not lead to socio-economically inefficient environmental degradation.

This finding is consistent with the above reported stylized facts that MNEs are generally more polluting in developing countries than they are at home, but less so than corresponding domestic firms. With firm-specific advantages in, for example, technology, management etc., and an experience of operations in industrialized countries, MNEs should have a lower marginal cost curve for pollution abatement than the domestic firms in a developing country. Moreover, given the plausible assumption that the social valuation of environmental protection increases with the level of income, developing host countries require a lower marginal cost for pollution abatement than industrialized home countries. The result is that MNEs are more polluting in the host country than they are at home, but less so than domestic firms.

It can be noted that home countries, like host countries, do not generally set an indiscriminate standard of protection, but bargain with individual firms. We can therefore ask whether the level of cleaning at home is restricted by a firm's opportunity to move abroad. By analogy with the above analysis, the answer is no. The level of home country earnings is restricted by an MNE's possibility to move abroad, just as the earnings of a host country are restricted by those that could be achieved in another country. The form of the earnings, however, is determined in a trade-off between taxation and environmental protection. Again, the costs of cleaning should not deviate from the social benefits at the margin.

Summing up, host countries require as much taxation and pollution control as possible without losing direct investment to their competitors. The marginal cost of pollution abatement should equal the marginal social benefit of forgoing environmental degradation. Thus, the outcome can be expected to be socially optimal. Of course, this result hinges on the assumption that there are no imperfections in the model. In practice, information may be incomplete and agents do not always behave in an economically rational manner. Nevertheless, we only have to worry about such objections to the extent that they suggest systematic influences, a matter returned to later. Before that we consider the implications for the pattern of pollution intensive direct investment.

THE PATTERN OF DIRECT INVESTMENT

In recent decades, new laws, regulations and private efforts in industrialized countries have enforced stricter environmental protection, which has led to higher costs for pollution intensive industries. This might be expected to give rise to a diffusion of such activities to developing countries where there is relatively less environmental protection. Following Walter (1972), Pearson (1976) forecast that international differences in environmental control costs would change the volume and composition of international investment flows. He predicted that the greater the differences in environmental control costs, the less spatially tied industries are to inputs or markets, and the more successful past foreign operations have been, the greater is the amount of relocation.

A number of empirical studies have examined to what extent prophesies such as these have been realized. Walter (1975) found some firm-level evidence of relocation of activities to developing countries when projects had been blocked at home for environmental reasons, but no evidence at the aggregate level that the pattern of direct investment would have been seriously affected by environmental considerations. Later studies, by Duerksen (1983) and Leonard (1984, 1988), for example, have not found much relocation motivated by environmental control costs. The effects that have been found relate primarily to two industries, those producing highly toxic products such as asbestos, benzidine dyes and pesticides, and those producing heavy metals such as copper, zinc and lead. In both these industries, new investment has tended to be located in developing countries when plants are closed in industrialized countries.

On the whole, there is relatively little evidence of environmentally motivated relocation of pollution intensive investment to countries with little environmental protection. This has puzzled some observers. One response has been that 'environmental control costs do not matter'. Gladwin and Welles (1976) expressed scepticism concerning the potential for relocation, arguing that the elasticity of investment is low with respect to environmental control costs. Requirements of pollution abatement would not represent a sufficiently large cost shift for most MNEs to motivate relocation. Leonard (1984) argued that pollution intensive industries have adapted to environmental regulations by developing technological innovations rather than by relocating across national boundaries. Pearson and Pryor (1978), however, maintained that the issue remains controversial until definite empirical estimates of environmentally induced shifts in location appear. It should also be emphasized that most studies have dealt only with flows of investment up to the early 1980s, whereas in many industrialized countries pollution control did not become mandatory until the late 1980s. Since it may take some time to relocate activities, it is possible that the 1990s will see larger effects of environmental control costs on the pattern of direct investment.

There is a close correlation between the stringency of environmental policy and income level (gross domestic product per capita (GDP/c)). Meanwhile, most direct investment in the developing world is obtained by the relatively high income 'newly industrialized countries', in which environmental protection has been growing the most.[5] While this state confuses a simple comparison between the location of investment and the level of environmental protection, it is compatible with our notion that countries bargain on the basis of the attractiveness of their investment opportunities. In our framework, differences in host country earnings are the natural outcome of competition between dissimilar countries, while the inter-country differences in environmental protection reflect differences in the social value of pollution. The outcome does not give rise to any relocation of direct investment from countries with superior investment opportunities to those with less favourable ones. On the contrary, host country competition realizes that the country with the best investment opportunities is the one which obtains a project.

Given our assumptions, environmental effects influence the location of direct investment only to the extent that they alter the relative valuation of a project among potential host countries. In terms of the goods–bads box in Figure 2.1, the net of the horizontal and vertical dimensions of the box in two potential host countries change place. Another country can afford to offer an MNE the largest profit net of tax and pollution abatement costs. Such a change must stem from differences either in the assimilative capacity of the environment or in the valuation of given effects.

It is sometimes argued that developing countries are natural waste baskets for pollution. Faced with serious and acute problems requiring urgent investment, such as hunger, illiteracy, unemployment, rural–urban imbalances, chronic poverty etc., these countries simply could not afford environmental protection. Ecological balance would be a luxury not affordable at the present level of development. Owing to their many urgent needs, the socially optimal level of environmental protection would be lower in developing countries than in industrialized countries.

However, it cannot be taken for granted that the developing countries would constitute the optimal location for pollution intensive activities. In particular, there is no conclusive evidence that the developing countries would have a relatively high assimilative capacity for pollutants. The assimilative capacity of the environment may or may not be relatively larger in developing countries. A hot dry climate may reduce the impact of some effluents, high rainfall reduces the impact on air quality etc., but temperature industrial countries have a higher assimilative capacity than tropical developing countries for other effluents. Many biological and chemical compounds spread more easily in the latter, people are less resistant to diseases etc.

In addition, pollution may reduce the quality of productive resources such as physical capital, labour productivity, land etc. Owing to their limited capacity to cope with such problems and the absence of safeguards, this generally poses a greater threat to developing countries than to industrialized countries. Consequently, there are many examples of 'horror stories' of environmental catastrophes in developing countries: accidents at chemical industries leading to thousands of casualties, the stripping of forests causing permanent destruction of land, phosphate mining making entire islands uninhabitable etc. Moreover, industries tend to be spatially concentrated in developing countries, and further expansion is likely to be undispersed. The possible counter-argument that the pollution intensity would be lower in industrial centres in developing countries than in the industrialized countries seldom holds any longer. Rather, the situation is the opposite today.

Thus, the assimilative capacity argument does not support an indiscriminate transfer of pollutants to developing countries, even if they may favour a transfer of certain pollutants. The differences in the valuation of environmental quality may motivate some additional transfer, but not when the outcome is a diminished productive capacity for the host country.[6] In any case, the scanty evidence that is currently available regarding relocation of direct investment from industrialized to developing countries may indicate that the net effect of the differences in assimilative capacity and the valuation of environmental impact does not generally alter the ranking of countries in terms of investment opportunities.

Summing up, the country with the best investment opportunities is the one which offers the most favourable conditions for an MNE and therefore obtains a project. Environmental effects influence the pattern of direct investment only to the extent that their impact on the net value of a project is sufficient to alter the ranking of potential host countries. The reasoning hinges on the absence of imperfections in the model. In the next section we discuss factors which are believed to be important for explaining deviations from the model results in the real world.

FACTORS AFFECTING THE MODEL RESULTS

By applying the model framework developed in Chapter 3 to pollution intensive direct investment, we have seen that the inclusion of external economies does not fundamentally alter the nature of the results obtained. Competition between potential host countries for gains from direct investment still produces an 'efficient' outcome. The host country which yields the highest net value of investment secures the project, and the cost of pollution abatement equals the benefit of preventing further environmental degradation at the margin.

We have already stated that our findings are consistent with certain general observations regarding pollution intensive direct investment in the real world. Relatively little relocation of pollution intensive activities has so far been observed: the level of cleaning employed by MNEs in developing countries is lower than in the industrialized countries, but higher than that of domestic firms, etc. At the same time, however, the real world does display a number of serious deviations from the model results. In many developing countries the required pollution control is not just low, but non-existent. Certainly, the social benefit of pollution abatement is hardly zero in any country. Moreover, many developing countries experience overwhelming environmental problems today, partly because of pollution from industrial processes. The air quality in Mexico City, Beijing or Taipei, or the irreversible destruction of rain forests in Indonesia, Central Africa and Latin America, hardly bear witness to socially optimal environmental protection.

In order to put the validity of our model results into perspective, in this section we discuss three sets of factors which may affect their realization in the real world: imperfections in international capital markets, imperfections in information and 'government failure'.

Imperfections in international capital markets

The marginal cost of environmental protection to the host country should be equal to the social scarcity cost of foreign exchange. However, imperfections in the international capital markets may prevent the latter from being 'internationally efficient'.[7] As shown by Eaton and Gersovitz (1981), Sachs and Cohen (1982) and Sachs (1984), for example, the existence of credit rationing can be explained in terms of the risk of debt repudiation, limited taxing power of the debtor country government over national wealth and imperfections related to the supply of loans (such as the risk of panic among creditors). As will be seen in Chapters 5–7, host country policies that interfere with the ownership of affiliates may similarly impede direct investment. Other factors that contribute to scarce capital are debt burdens accumulated when interest rates were low and that require increased payments as a result of higher interest rates, budget deficits and soaring inflation causing overvalued exchange rates, barriers to imports from developing countries in industrialized countries etc.

Owing to such factors, many developing countries are today stuck with a marginal rate of return to capital which is higher than it is in the rest of the world. Viewed from a global perspective, this represents an inefficient allocation of resources. The countries in question value capital too highly compared with the case of a perfect capital market.

Imperfections in information

It has been assumed that the cost and social benefit of pollution abatement are equal at the margin. In practice, there may be imperfections in information concerning both the costs and the social benefits of cleaning. In particular, it may be extremely difficult to identify, quantify and evaluate the environmental effects. The developing countries have relatively limited technical, economic and administrative expertise to trace effects, or to check compliance with pollution control. Some developing countries have passed fairly rigorous environmental laws, but they are seldom enforced. Owing to their relative lack of resources for information gathering, the developing countries can be said to suffer greater environmental risks than the industrialized countries.

An individual's perspective on risk may differ from that of all individuals in a society together. Under fairly strict assumptions, Arrow and Lind (1970) argued that, if risks are borne by the government, risk-spreading implies that society should be risk-neutral. This suggests that the risk for an unexpected outcome need not affect the choice of discount rate. In reality, imperfect risk-spreading may violate this proposition. The willingness of risk-averse individuals to pay extra in order to retain certain options for the future can theoretically be represented by an 'option value' (Weisbroad 1964). Option values may be either positive or negative, however, and may affect the valuation of environmental effects in either direction.

More straightforward implications follow from a lack of markets which relate future environmental goods and services to current values. In the developing countries, the major enviornmental concern is the economic productivity of ecological systems (cf. Freeman 1979; Bojö *et al.* 1990). An environmental impact tends to ascend through ecological chains, and materialize with a time lag. The ecological systems typically constitute imperfectly known resources, taking the form of collective goods or factors of production so that private incentives for their preservation are hampered. We can assess a 'quasi-option value' for the irreversible destruction of currently unknown values (cf. Fisher 1981). However, it is impossible to assign a precise estimate to this value.[8]

Concerning the valuation of environmental effects there are, first, difficulties in accurately estimating recreation values, option values and bequest values, for example, which are not automatically articulated in markets.[9] In developing countries, such values tend to be neglected. Second, future consumer preferences are unknown today. Third, environmental preferences are often unstable, and may adjust in either direction with improved information.

Government failure

A government which maximizes social welfare over a sufficiently long time horizon could account for socio-economically optimal investment in the provision of information on environmental degradation. Remaining risks that could not be taken care of by insurance markets should, ideally, be reflected in option values and quasi-option values. Adjustments could be made to take account of an expected future upgrading of consumer preferences for environmental quality. In practice, governments in the Third World have proved not to be much more inclined than private agents to spend resources on investigating or preventing environmental degradation.

This brings us to the matter of 'government failure'. With the school of public choice, it has become widely questioned whether economics and politics can be separated. A government need not maximize social welfare, but may act according to a self-interest which differs from that of society as a whole. Because a society is not made up of homogeneous households, regimes (whether autocratic or democratic) may choose to base power on certain influential groups rather than other less articulate ones.

Like other social costs and benefits, environmental impacts affect households or individuals unevenly. The acceptance of environmental degradation incorporates an inherent decision regarding the distribution of cuts in individual welfare. This can be made less painful politically by targeting the effects on groups that are the least likely to be aware of, and/or protest about, their exposure to environmental risk. One aspect of this problem is the prevention of free publication and criticism of environmental mismanagement. In particular, societies without free elections tend to prevent competing movements from capitalizing on the need for changes in public intervention to prevent environmental degradation (Bojö *et al.* 1990). In contrast, politicians seeking to maximize their self-interest can readily make use of foreign exchange earnings.

Imperfections in the international capital markets, imperfections in information and/or 'government failure' may upgrade the value of foreign exchange relative to environmental protection. Since host countries set environmental protection in a direct trade-off with 'taxation', it is likely that many countries choose to capture 'too much' of their gains from direct investment as foreign exchange earnings, and allow 'too much' pollution. Of course, a country which downgrades environmental quality relatively more than other competing countries may attract direct investment, although the net value of such investment is not at a maximum in this country. In this case, the outcome is an investment pattern which runs contrary to an efficient inter-country allocation of resources. As has been made clear, such an outcome does not derive from host country competition *per se*, and it is not inherent in the behaviour of countries *vis-à-vis* MNEs. The causes are to be found in factors such as those discussed in this section, and the resulting bias against pollution control applies to more or less all economic activities, whether domestic or foreign owned.

SUMMARY AND CONCLUSIONS

Applying the model framework developed in Chapter 3, we have analysed host country competition for pollution intensive investment projects. The inclusion of external economies has not affected the basic nature of the results obtained in that chapter. The net gain of a host country still depends on the quality of its investment opportunities in relation to the second best country and the mobility of investment projects. The new element is that a host country must decide in what proportion to earn foreign exchange (through 'taxation') and in what proportion to prevent pollution ('environmental protection').

We have seen that competition between host countries does not induce a suboptimal level of environmental protection. Moreover, differences in environmental protection, like differences in taxation between countries, do not influence the location of direct investment unless they reflect differences in the assimilative capacity of pollution or in the valuation of given effects. Whether developing countries do represent the optimal location for pollution intensive activities is an open question.

The limited relocation of such activities observed in practice may indicate that this is not generally the case.

The model results are consistent with many observations in the real world. For example, the level of cleaning employed by MNEs in developing countries is lower than it is in the home country but higher than that of domestic firms. Nevertheless, there are deviations, such as a complete absence of environmental protection and an excessive amount of environmental degradation in many developing countries. The plausible reasons are to be found in imperfections in the international capital markets, imperfections in information and 'government failure'.

The findings may make it seem ill advised to opt for international co-operation regarding environmental policies *vis-à-vis* MNEs, as is currently done through the Organization for Economic Co-operation and Development (OECD) and the United Nations.[10] One counter-argument is that we have not dealt with pollution that affects resources that are common to many countries. Leaving this out, a forced inter-nalization of the costs for pollution within the polluting firms world-wide may still be motivated by the gains of speeding up the development and spread of environmental management. As with taxation in general, however, interference with environmental protection is not motivated by host country competition *per se*. On the contrary, this serves to achieve an efficient pattern of direct investment. Rather than striving for universal standards, for example, a possible interference with pollution abatement could seek to establish it on the basis of a social evaluation of the costs and benefits. Polluters, whether domestic or foreign should be confronted with the costs that they inflict in a particular environment.

Part III

Nationalization of multinational enterprise affiliates

5 Nationalization of multinational enterprise affiliates by competing host countries

INTRODUCTION

It is widely believed that international capital flows may be impeded or distorted by the behaviour of capital-importing countries. For example, Eaton and Gersovitz (1981) showed that the risk of debt repudiation may constrain a country's international borrowing. In Chapter 3 we suggested that taxation of MNE affiliates should not prevent or distort their undertaking direct investment when there is effective competition between potential host countries. We now turn to the other policy option dealt with in this study, i.e. nationalization.

There have been many studies of nationalization over the years, including those by Knudsen (1974), Moran (1974), Truitt (1974), Williams (1975), Jodice (1980), Kobrin (1980), Sigmund (1980), Burton and Inoue (1984) and Juhl (1985). While the role of political motives is fairly clear, at least for so-called mass nationalization, there is considerable uncertainty concerning the economic motives. This is unsatisfactory since economic factors seem to have become of great importance from the late 1960s with the rapid increase in selective nationalization (cf. Chapter 1).

Theoretical studies dealing with economic motives for nationalization tend to be concerned with the effects of the risk of the policy, rather than explaining when it would be likely actually to occur. In models with complete information, the occurrence of nationalization tends to be ruled out since rational firms do not invest in the first place if they know that they are to be nationalized. Eaton and Gersovitz (1983) can be said to suggest that nationalization is more likely when there is a high rate of discounting and plenty of domestic capital. Meanwhile, Eaton and Gersovitz (1984) explain nationalization as random variation, suggesting that it would be stochastic in nature and not possible to relate to any systematic factors. However, neither of these explanations is very helpful when confronted with the real world. As will be seen in Chapters 6 and 7, empirical studies have similarly had limited success in explaining when nationalization occurs. It is still unclear whether, for example, the policy is pursued at 'good times or bad times'. As long as the reasons for and the timing of nationalization by host countries remain unknown, we can at best speculate on the effects.

In this chapter we present theoretical models of nationalization. Our aims are first, to establish the circumstances under which host countries nationalize MNE affiliates and, second, to derive conclusions regarding welfare effects and policy implications. We assume that the benefits of nationalization stem from the retention of profits that cannot be taxed. Concerning costs, there is a distinction between direct costs, relating to the MNE targeted, and indirect costs associated with other agents. The direct costs here constitute a reduction of profits owing to the loss of the parent's ownership-specific advantages. In practice, there may also be reduced spin-off effects on domestic firms. The value depends on the technology of MNEs and host countries. As previously stated, in this study indirect costs are considered only to the extent that they materialize through direct or portfolio investment. As far as this chapter is concerned, we are limited to indirect effects on the undertakings of direct investment. In Chapter 3 it was suggested that the direct effects (costs) of taxation are normally sufficient to rule out a prevention of direct investment. With nationalization, we need to consider both direct and indirect costs.

In relation to previous work on nationalization, this chapter introduces at least three novel points. First, it is considered that host countries may nationalize projects on a random basis. Second, we explicitly model the discouraging effect of nationalization on direct investment. Third, we analyse nationalization not only by a single country, but also by countries which compete for gains from direct investment. This makes it necessary to consider co-ordination problems in host countries' behaviour.

The outline of the chapter is as follows. First we analyse the direct and indirect costs of nationalization. We move from complete information to incomplete information and trigger strategy equilibria. We then assume that a host country may play mixed strategies, there randomizing which firms are nationalized. It is shown that a mixed strategy equilibrium containing nationalization is compatible with the continued undertaking of direct investment. Next we introduce a two-country framework and allow firm-specific profits from direct investment, and we analyse the circumstances under which one or both countries nationalize. It is demonstrated that there are two subgame perfect equilibria which are unique for given parameter values. In one, both countries nationalize and in the other, no country does. Finally we investigate the factors that determine equilibria and may cause shifts between them. The chapter is summarized and concluded in the last section.

DIRECT AND INDIRECT COSTS OF NATIONALIZATION

Again, assume that direct investment requires sunk costs and that profits represent the entire value of production. The scale of a subsidiary is given by technology and its life span is represented by one time period, after which it depreciates completely. An MNE is taken to be risk-neutral and to maximize its overall profit net of tax. Given an exempt tax system at home, a subsidiary maximizes its return net of tax to the host country. With a risk of nationalization, it maximizes expected profit net of tax.

In Chapter 3, host country competition limited the optimal level of taxation because of the MNEs' capacity to relocate subsidiaries and/or produce elsewhere. The analysis was directly concerned only with export-oriented investment, for which nationalization is often less of a threat since the parent's access to foreign markets tends to be crucial for profitability. As noted in Chapter 2, however, there is also some host country competition for import-substituting direct investment. Moreover, a host country's ability to tax a foreign-owned subsidiary may be limited by the opportunities open to an MNE to use transfer price manipulations and by indirect effects such as the costs of damaging an ongoing business relationship.[1]

A limitation on what a host country can accomplish through taxation is the point of departure for this chapter. We denote the host country's corporate income tax by ϕ, which is such that $\phi \epsilon [0, 1]$. This is viewed as exogenously determined and fixed at the 'optimal' level where the host country's tax revenue is maximized, meaning that a further increase in ϕ does not generate larger host country earnings. Firms are left with a minimum share $1 - \phi$. In other words, host countries maximize tax revenue but may still be unable to tax all profit. Compare this with the notion of a 'Laffer curve' in tax income. By nationalizing, the host country may be able to do better.

To begin with a simple case, assume complete information and that one MNE contemplates whether to invest in a single host country only once. The game is illustrated in extensive form in Figure 5.1. If the MNE does not invest, both the MNE and the host country earn zero. If it does invest, the host country chooses whether or not to nationalize. In the event of nationalization, the MNE loses the sunk cost S, while the host country earns the whole profit (π^N) under domestic ownership. In the case of

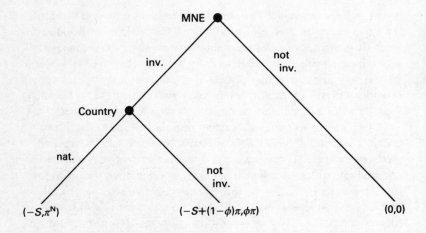

Figure 5.1 One-firm–one-country game (in extensive form)

no nationalization, the MNE earns profit net of tax minus the sunk cost while the host country earns tax income $(\phi\pi)$ from the foreign-run operations.

Figure 5.2 illustrates the outcome in coalitional form. The utility of the MNE is measured along the horizontal axis, and the host country's is measured along the vertical. The candiates for equilibria are marked by full points and bold lines. We have the points $(u_F, u_C) = (0,0)$ and $(u_F, u_C) = (-S, \pi^N)$ and the diagonal line above the horizontal axis. The point $(u_F, u_C) = (0,0)$ represents the case when investment is not undertaken, and $(-S, \pi^N)$ represents the case of nationalization. Since the parent company's ownership advantages are lost with nationalization, we have $\pi^N \leqslant \pi$, where the difference represents the direct cost. The MNE makes a loss in this case, since we are to the left of the vertical axis. Finally, the diagonal line shows the possible outcomes of operations under foreign ownership. The upper left-hand end point is achieved by $\phi = 1$, while $\phi = 0$ places us in the lower right-hand corner. An outcome below the horizontal axis is not possible since a negative tax has been ruled out.

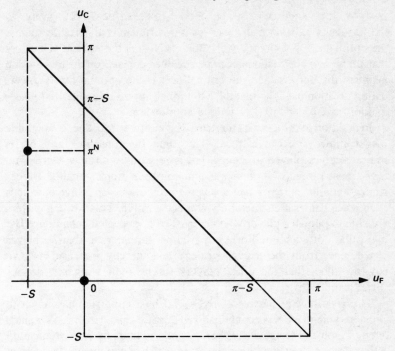

Figure 5.2 One-firm–one-country game (in coalitional form)

Equilibrium is determined by solving the game by backward induction. If $\phi > 1 - S/\pi$, we are along the diagonal line to the left of the vertical axis in Figure 5.2, meaning that the tax is too high to allow the MNE to cover its sunk cost. Given that this is not the case, the undertaking of direct investment depends on whether taxation or nationalization renders the largest earnings for the host country. The condition for ruling out nationalization is

$$\phi \pi \geqslant \pi^N \qquad (5.1)$$

We do not require a strict inequality, but assume that the host country abstains from nationalization if it earns as much from taxation. The critical tax, i.e. the lowest rate of tax that prevents nationalization from paying, is consequently

$$\phi^* = \pi^N / \pi \qquad (5.2)$$

The critical tax ϕ^* must be distinguished from the optimal tax ϕ discussed above. As can be seen from (5.2), the critical tax is given by the direct cost. With no such cost, so that $\pi^N = \pi$, the critical tax is unity. In that case nationalization always pays if investment is undertaken, unless the optimal tax is unity as well. When $\pi^N \neq \pi$, the critical tax is less than unity. Whether nationalization is pursued depends on the relationship between the optimal and the critical tax. If the optimal tax is lower, nationalization pays, so that the MNE does not invest in the first place, making $(u_F, u_C) = (0,0)$ a unique equilibrium.[2]

In addition to direct costs there may be indirect costs due to a possible loss of future direct investment. The game illustrated in Figure 5.1 is in practice not played just once, but is repeated with new MNEs and investment projects. In games containing repetition, so-called trigger strategy equilibria may enable players to achieve co-operative outcomes even when games are structurally non-cooperative. This is when players are able to punish a player who deviates from expected behaviour. The two pillars of such equilibria are credible threats, and that no player can deviate from the trigger strategy and thereby increase his own pay-off given that the other players follow their trigger strategies (Friedman 1986).

The relationship between MNEs and host countries has much in common with that between international creditors and debtors. As pointed out by Eaton and Gersovitz (1981), private creditors may take retaliatory actions to penalize defaulting debtors, of which one of the most important is exclusion from future borrowing. They assume that a country which fails to honour its implicit debt contract tarnishes its reputation and is cut off from international capital markets for ever. Likewise, granted incomplete information concerning countries' pay-off functions, but a notion of different kinds of host countries, a country may establish its character by nationalizing. MNEs can then pursue the strategy not to invest in a country which has nationalized (cf. Eaton and Gersovitz 1983).

Assume that the game in Figure 5.1 is repeated for one potential investment project in each period. For convenience, we associate an MNE with one investment project and assume that the profit level is the same for all direct investment. A country that nationalizes ruins its reputation and cannot attract MNEs thereafter. If the time horizon is finite, the problem is trivial. In the case when nationalization pays with respect to an individual project, it pays in the last time period. Since this is known beforehand, an MNE does not invest in that period, making the second last the last in which investment is contemplated, and so on back to the start of the game. Thus the outcome does not differ from the one-period game. If the time horizon is infinite, however, there is no last time period. It is then possible to achieve a trigger strategy equilibrium.[3] In accordance with Friedman (1986) the condition for such an equilibrium, with no nationalization, can be determined as a limitation on the discount factor. Nationalization enables a country to retain the whole profit under domestic ownership, but MNEs pursue the strategy never to invest in a country which has nationalized. If the country does not nationalize, it earns taxes from direct investment over an infinite time horizon. Setting up the two alternatives as a sum of revenue terms and comparing the outcome, we obtain the condition for nationalization not to pay as

$$\frac{\phi\pi}{1-\delta} \geqslant \pi^N + \frac{0}{1-\delta} \tag{5.3}$$

where δ is the discount factor, delimited by $\delta \epsilon [0,1]$. Expression (5.3) states that collecting taxes over an infinite time horizon must be at least as rewarding as nationalizing everything today and obtaining zero tax revenue for ever after. By rearranging (5.3) we obtain

$$\delta \geqslant 1 - \frac{\pi\phi}{\pi^N} \tag{5.4}$$

as the condition for continued investment flows. If the discount factor is so low that (5.4) is violated, the host country's future tax earnings forgone are too small to outweigh the gain of nationalizing today. As can be seen, nationalization is prevented by combinations of sufficiently high taxes and discount rates. By inserting (5.2) in (5.4), the latter is seen to be equivalent to

$$\delta \geqslant 1 - \frac{\phi}{\phi^*} \tag{5.5}$$

The combinations of ϕ and δ which exactly prevent nationalization from paying form a straight line, or boundary, with an intercept $\delta = 1$ and a negative slope as illustrated in Figure 5.3. When $\pi/\pi^N = 1$, so that there is no direct cost from nationalization, the right-hand side in (5.5) is $1 - \phi$, and the slope of the boundary is -1. The greater the direct cost, the larger is π/π^N, the smaller is ϕ^* and the greater is the slope. The field in which nationalization pays shrinks. In the extreme case when $\phi^* = 0$, the boundary is vertical and nationalization does not pay no matter how small the discount factor and the optimal tax.

Thus, we have seen the combinations of direct and indirect costs that prevent nationalization when the time horizon is infinite and information is incomplete. But how useful is this kind of trigger strategy equilibrium

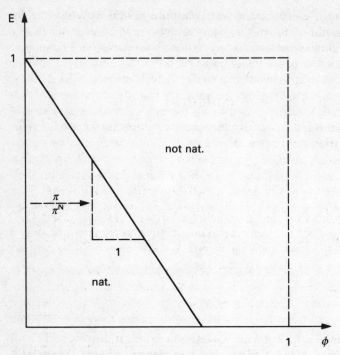

Figure 5.3   Nationalization in trigger equilibria

as an explanation of real world phenomena? It should be noted that the application of equilibria based on reputation effects for explaining international borrowing has been questioned by, for example, Bulow and Rogoff (1989b). Since reputation models neglect the ability of countries to bargain, they may overstate the possibility of cutting off a country from world capital markets. Equilibria based on trigger strategies played by MNEs *vis-à-vis* host countries can be subject to similar counter-arguments. In practice, nationalization does not damage a country's reputation altogether, but a great deal of investment continues to be undertaken. In particular, this applies to selective nationalization, which has often been accompanied by endeavours to attract new investment. The historical record suggests that MNEs act as individual agents and do not formulate strategies collectively. If a host country has nationalized a subsidiary, an MNE that contemplates direct investment in the future does not abstain from direct investment if it still expects a non-negative profit.

The notion of trigger strategy equilibria highlights that it is not the occurrence but the risk of nationalization which matters. With effective trigger strategies, the policy is never observed. We argue that a satisfactory theory of nationalization must incorporate an explanation of when it does occur.

MIXED STRATEGY EQUILIBRIUM

Again, nationalization does not occur if a firm knows that it is to be nationalized if it invests. However, the host country has the option to play mixed strategies, taking over a share of direct investment while randomizing the specific targets. An individual firm must then calculate the probability that it will be targeted if it invests. This probability is equivalent to the share of investment nationalized by the host country. This construction, which may not seem wholly realistic, reflects the uncertainty perceived by individual firms in the real world.

Assume that there is a large supply of potential investment projects each period. The level of profits π is the same for all projects, but is negatively related to the number undertaken. Nevertheless, we assume $\pi \geqslant s/(1 - \phi)$ over the intervals dealt with, so that there are real gains to be obtained from additional projects. The profits subsequent to nationalization on the other hand are determined by a host country's technology and entrepreneurial capacity. We assume $\pi^N > \phi \pi$, which must be fulfilled if nationalization is to be considered at all, but view π^N as given and fixed at a level below π.[4]

Firms do not form strategies collectively, but each firm sets up a subsidiary if and only if

$$u_F = S + \pi (1 - \phi)(1 - \lambda) - 0 \lambda \geqslant 0 \qquad (5.6)$$

where S is the sunk cost required for direct investment, π is the pre-tax profit and λ is the risk of nationalization, which takes a number $\lambda \in [0, 1]$. Expression (5.6) says that an MNE weighs its profit after tax with the probability of not being nationalized, and invests only if the expected profit u_F is non-negative. If (5.6) does not hold, the profit net of tax is not large enough to cover the sunk cost and compensate for the risk λ, so that direct investment is prevented in the first place. The host country, on the other hand, maximizes the discounted value of its earnings from direct investment at every point in time over an infinite time horizon. Viewed from time t, this can be written

$$\max_{\lambda} u_C = \sum_{t=1}^{\infty} \delta^{t-1} n_t [\lambda_t \pi_t^N + (1 - \lambda_t) \pi_t \phi_t] \qquad (5.7)$$

where n is the number of projects actually undertaken each period. Equation (5.7) states that the host country earns the whole profit under domestic ownership from nationalized direct investment $n\lambda$ (where λ is equivalent to the probability that the host country nationalizes a specific investment project) and tax revenue from investment which is not nationalized $n (1 - \lambda)$.

In the following, we build on the notion of a reputation effect of nationalization, and again apply the concept of a trigger strategy equilibrium. However, MNEs are taken to form their strategies individually in the sense that a firm views a country as destroying its reputation only when a continuation of its present behaviour reduces the firm's expected profitability below zero. Direct investment is consequently prevented from being undertaken only when (5.6) is violated.

Furthermore, assume that $\partial u_C / \partial \lambda > 0$ as long as (5.6) holds. This requires that n falls sufficiently slowly over the relevant intervals. Two main choices can then be identified for the host country: 'optimal selective' nationalization and 'mass' nationalization. In the former, the host country nationalizes the greatest share of direct investment which allows (5.6) to be satisfied. To nationalize less is suboptimal. In the latter case, the host country nationalizes everything, i.e. $\lambda = 1$, since it is optimal to nationalize everything once (5.6) is violated. By analogy with (5.3), the condition for ruling out mass nationalization (rendering 'optimal selective' nationalization superior to 'mass') is

$$n \left[\frac{\lambda \pi^N}{1 - \delta} + \frac{1 - \lambda) \, \phi \pi}{1 - \delta]} \right] \geqslant n \left(\frac{\pi^N + 0}{1 - \delta} \right) \tag{5.8}$$

which states that nationalizing $n\lambda$ investment projects and collecting tax revenue from $n(1 - \lambda)$ projects over an infinite time horizon must be at least as rewarding as nationalizing n projects today and earning zero for ever after. By rearranging (5.8) we obtain

$$\delta \geqslant (1 - \lambda) \left(1 - \frac{\pi \phi}{\pi^N} \right) \tag{5.9}$$

as a limitation on which discount factor is compatible with selective nationalization. Expression (5.9) is analogous to (5.4), from which it differs only by the inclusion of $1 - \lambda$.

The unique solution is obtained by setting (5.6) equal to zero and inserting the obtained π in (5.9) written as an equality. By rearranging, we have

$$\lambda^* = 1 - \delta - \frac{S\,\phi}{\pi^N(1 - \phi)} \qquad (5.10)$$

in equilibrium. λ^* is the share of direct investment nationalized each period over an infinite time horizon. This represents a mixed strategy equilibrium based on sequential rationality on the part of each player. It is equivalent to the subgame perfect equilibrium due to Selten (1975) (cf. Kreps and Wilson 1982). The reason is that, in each period, firms undertake direct investment as long as the host country does not completely jeopardize its reputation, i.e. nationalizes sufficiently little direct investment not to make a continuation of the policy reduce firms' expected profits below zero. Investment projects keep coming until π has been sufficiently depressed to realize (5.10).[5] It is common knowledge that the host country then does the best it can by nationalizing the share λ^* of investment. If additional projects came in, the level of expected profits would become negative. There is no way that any player can increase his pay-off by deviating from this equilibrium.

The result that mass nationalization cannot occur in equilibrium, while selective nationalization can, is consistent with the observations in Chapter 1 that the former is politically motivated and the latter is pursued independently of ideology. As can be seen from (5.10), the optimal amount of selective nationalization is larger, the higher the rate of discounting (the smaller the value of future investment), the lower the tax rate (the weaker the best alternative to nationalization), the smaller the sunk cost and the higher the profit subsequent to nationalization. Note that the condition for no nationalizations to occur has already been given in (5.4).

Regarding optimal selective nationalization, we have seen that there is a continued flow of investment. However, the flow is 'rationed' as the level of profit required for direct investment to be undertaken is higher the greater the share which is nationalized selectively. Thus, the risk of nationalization discourages some direct investment from being undertaken. Potential mutual profits for MNEs and host countries are forgone, which provides a *raison d'être* for interference in the market. However, the size of the welfare losses is indeterminate without knowledge of how much direct investment is actually discouraged.

To summarize, in this section we have determined a mixed strategy equilibrium for a single country when investment projects generate the same profit. Direct investment is motivated in each period until the expected profits of MNEs have been reduced to zero at the limit where mass nationalization is exactly ruled out. Some direct investment may be prevented from being undertaken because of the risk of nationalization, which provides a *raison d'être* for interference in the market.

A weakness of the above analysis is that no real consideration is given to the opportunity costs of MNEs, which prevents any determination of how much direct investment is discouraged by selective nationalization. To account for this, we need an explicit formulation of the distribution of profits among different investment projects. In the next section, we allow firms to be dissimilar, so that their expected rate of return after tax varies. In addition, we include two host countries which compete for gains from direct investment. Because firms may have different countries to choose between, the discouraging effect of nationalization in one country is influenced by the behaviour of the other. Determining the behaviour of competing host countries is the task addressed in the rest of this chapter.

FRAMEWORK OF TWO-COUNTRY COMPETITION

The best alternative available to an MNE which contemplates undertaking direct investment in one country is often to undertake the investment in another similar country. This opens up the possibility of competition between potential host countries. Minor (1988) wrote that 'it appears important to examine host country behaviour in a global context rather than simply in terms of a host country–multinational investor dyad'. That there have been no previous investigations of the role of host country competition for nationalization may depend on the complexity of the set-up and its sensitivity to arbitrary assumptions. Rather than developing a taxonomy of possibilities, we choose a set-up which is believed to be representative of a wide range of outcomes. Our aim is to demonstrate some plausible outcomes. The model specification is crucial for the exact results, but similar implications follow from other possible constructions.

Consider two potential host countries A and B. As in the previous section, we assume that reputation effects link periods so that mass nationalization is prevented in each country. We simplify by viewing the number of possible investment projects in each period as a finite and given number which stops short of the level where mass nationalization pays. We abstain from determining how the profit level among firms is influenced by the flow of investment, and instead focus on dissimilarities in profitability between investment projects. Such differences make them differentially sensitive to the risk of nationalization.[6] Comparing the two countries, each MNE invests where the highest positive pay-off is expected. The choice hinges on profits before tax π, tax rates ϕ and risks of nationalization λ. Our assumptions are as follows.

1 The pre-tax profit π varies between firms and possibly between countries. We assume that the profits in the two countries are characterized by a uniform distribution $\pi_A = [0, 1]$ and $\pi_B = [0, 1]$. The profit π_f of a specific project in one country may or may not be dependent on the profit of a similar project in the other country. The degree of dependence is measured by the parameter $\mu \, \epsilon \, [\, 1, \infty]$. When $\mu = 1$, the project's profits in the two countries are completely independent; when it goes to infinity there is perfect correlation. μ can be interpreted as an indicator of the extent to which the two countries are substitutes for direct investment.[7]

2 The tax rates ϕ are the same for all projects and are equal in the two countries.

3 The risk of nationalization is again equal to the share of investment which is nationalized. In practice, it is likely that a host country's choice stands between nationalizing a certain positive amount of investment, or not nationalizing at all. As demonstrated in the preceding section, the optimal nationalization intensity is restricted by the level where all direct investment is discouraged when projects generate the same profit. An upper limit may also be motivated by scarce entrepreneurial capacity in the host country, reducing π^N by the amount of direct investment taken. A lower limit may be motivated by the symbolic nature of nationalization, making investors pay great attention to whether the policy occurs at all (decreasing marginal indirect effects of nationalizing additional direct investment). Alternatively, there may be indivisiblities in the amount of investment which can be taken effectively.

For such reasons, a study of nationalization may focus on whether the policy occurs at all rather than the amount of investment which is taken. Thus, we consider here a country's dichotomous choice between whether to nationalize a certain proportion of direct investment or not to nationalize at all. That is, λ either takes a given exogenously determined positive value in one or both of the two countries, or it is zero. If a country chooses the former, it is said to play a mixed strategy; if it chooses the latter, it plays the pure strategy without any nationalization.

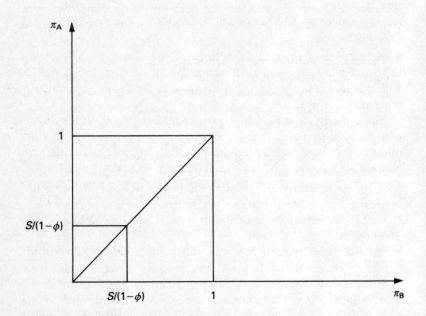

Figure 5.4   Distribution of profits in two countries

Figure 5.4 illustrates the distribution of MNEs' pre-tax profits from direct investment in the two countries. It shows the case $\pi_A = [0, 1]$, $\pi_B = [0, 1]$ and $\mu = 1$. The distribution of profits is uniform and independent in the two countries, so that there is an equal probability for a randomly selected firm to be positioned anywhere in the box. When there is no nationalization, so that $\lambda_A = \lambda_B = 0$, the probability that a specific investment project is not undertaken in either country is represented by the size of the smaller square in the lower left-hand corner ($S/(1 - \phi)$ multiplied by $S/(1 - \phi)$) relative to the whole 'box'. The reason for this is that a project with such profits in the two countries cannot cover its sunk cost with its profit net of tax in any country. The probability that an investment project is located in country A is represented by the rest of the triangle above the vertical 45° dividing line, and that of investment in country B is represented by the rest of the triangle below that line.

Assume that the host countries are aware of the distribution of profits among firms, but have incomplete information concerning the profitability of specific projects, which is known only by an MNE itself. This is assumed always to hold, so that there is no learning over time concerning this firm characteristic. The construction is motivated by, for example, intra-firm transactions and blurring of the profitability of affiliates by transfer pricing. In particular, it is difficult for a host country to know the profitability of specific projects in its own territory compared with that in another competing host country. See further comments at the end of the next section.

The interaction between the two countries is dealt with in terms of a non-cooperative game. Each country maximizes its gains from direct investment over an infinite time horizon, and must take into account the behaviour of the other country as well as that of the MNE. Figure 5.1 is applicable as an illustration in the extensive form of the game with respect to each MNE, with two qualifications. First, an MNE chooses between country A and B. Second, the countries either nationalize a certain part of the direct investment that they obtain, randomizing the policy, or they play the pure strategy of not nationalizing.

Whichever strategy is chosen, this is immediately known to all players. The expected profit net of tax in, say, country A must be weighed by an MNE with the probability that it is not nationalized there, which is $1 - \lambda_A$. If an MNE does not invest in any country, it earns zero; if it invests, it spends S. When projects have been established, the countries decide whether to play the pure strategy of not nationalizing, or to play the mixed strategy and nationalize the share λ of the investment. From nationalized subsidiaries, the host country earns π^N, which represents an expected average value, and forgoes $\phi\pi_f$, while MNEs lose their sunk costs. From subsidiaries which are not nationalized, the host country earns $\phi\pi_f$ and MNEs earn $(1 - \phi)\pi_f - S$.

The game is reiterated each period as n MNEs decide whether and where to invest. The two host countries maximize their discounted pay-offs over an infinite time horizon. Firms' investment decisions are influenced by the risk of nationalization in both countries. In equilibrium, each country either pursues a mixed strategy with selective nationalizations or plays the pure strategy with no nationalizations. In the next section we investigate what will prevail in a two-country equilibrium.

TWO-COUNTRY EQUILIBRIUM

Which form of nationalization behaviour is pursued by two countries which compete for gains from direct investment as outlined above? Two equilibrium concepts are used in the following: first, the Nash equilibrium, according to which all agents maximize their utility given the best response of all other agents; second, the subgame perfect equilibrium introduced by Selten (1975). A combination of strategies forms a subgame perfect equilibrium if, in every subgame, the strategies relating to that subgame are a Nash equilibrium.

Depending on whether one or both of the two countries nationalize in equilibrium, we have four possible outcomes with discounted pay-offs for the countries as shown in Table 5.1 where u denotes the discounted present value of changes in a country's utility relative to the state when both countries play the pure strategy without nationalization, superscript N stands for nationalization and superscript a stands for 'alone' – 'not nationalizing alone' or 'nationalizing alone'.

Table 5.1 Two-country pay-offs

	B not nationalized	B nationalized
A not nationalized	u_A, u_B	u_A^a, u_B^{Na}
A nationalized	u_A^{Na}, u_B^a	u_A^N, u_B^N

In the following, the most plausible outcomes are illustrated by a few numerical examples. From these we move on to the pay-off relations which determine equilibrium. Consider Table 5.2, which presents parameter values. Common values are given in the top row, while the lower rows present values that are specific for three numerical examples, denoted (i), (ii) and (iii). In all three, the distribution of profits in the two countries is independent and uniformly distributed between zero and unity, the sunk cost is 0.1 and the discount factor 0.5. In the first two, the countries are symmetrical. π^N is 0.3, and the share of investment nationalized takes a value of either zero or 0.2. Thus, the two countries choose between the pure strategy of not nationalizing at all and the mixed strategy of nationalizing 20 per cent of investment. The only difference between the first two examples is in the tax, which takes values of 0.2 and 0.5 respectively. As will be seen, these two illustrate the only equilibria that are possible when the countries are symmetrical. In (iii), π^N is higher in country B than in country A, which can be interpreted as country B's having a relatively greater capacity to run nationalized firms.

Table 5.2 Numerical example with two countries

$\pi_A = \pi_B = [0, 1]$	$S_A = S_B = 0.1$	$\delta = 0.5$	$\mu = 1$
(i) $\phi = 0.2$	$\lambda_A, \lambda_B \in \{0, 0.2\}$	$N_A = N_B = 0.3$	
(ii) $\phi = 0.5$	$\lambda_A, \lambda_B \in \{0, 0.2\}$	$N_A = N_B = 0.3$	
(iii) $\phi = 0.5$	$\lambda_A, \lambda_B \in \{0, 0.2\}$	$N_A = 0.3, N_B = 0.5$	

Consider Figure 5.5 for an illustration of the case when only country A plays the mixed strategy. The positive λ_A reduces the expected profit in this country. In the case when country B does not nationalize, projects in the area which is only negatively hatched do not find it worthwhile to invest in any country owing to the risk of nationalization in country A. Those in the positively hatched area are induced to locate in country B instead.[7] In the case when country B nationalizes as well, country A discourages projects in the area which is negatively hatched (which abstain from investing in either country). Country B then discourages a corresponding amount of investment.

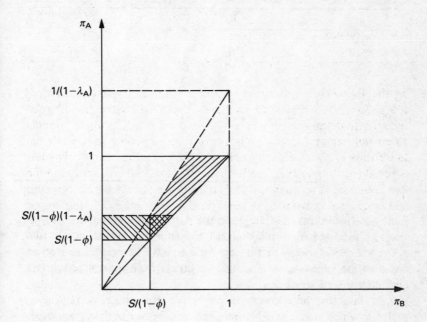

Figure 5.5 Nationalization in country A

With parameter values as in Table 5.2, the two countries obtain the three sets of approximate pay-offs given in Table 5.3. The figures represent the discounted pay-offs as a percentage of the pre-tax profit level of the average project, which is $\pi = 0.5$, relative to the case of no nationalization. Thus, we have zero pay-offs throughout in the first row, first column. In case (i), for example, a mixed strategy with $\lambda = 0.2$ in both countries results in an expected pay-off in both which is 16 per cent of the average value of production, as seen in the second row, second column. In case (ii), nationalization in country A only results in a 10 per cent lower pay-off in country A and a 14 per cent higher pay-off in country B, as seen from the second row, second column, since some investment projects are relocated to country B. Note that nationalization would occur in both countries throughout in the case of collusion. If any other outcome generated a higher total pay-off, nationalization could never pay in our framework. This is not to say that nationalization is socially preferable – an issue returned to below. Solving for equilibrium, this is as follows in the three examples.

Table 5.3 Pay-off to nationalization in two countries, normal form

	B (not N)		B$^{(N)}$	
Case (i)				
A$^{(not N)}$	0	0	6	10
A$^{(N)}$	10	6	16	16
Case (ii)				
A$^{(not N)}$	0	0	14	−10
A$^{(N)}$	−10	14	4	4
Case (iii)				
A$^{(not N)}$	0	0	14	6
A$^{(N)}$	−10	14	4	20

In case (i) the mixed strategy on the part of both countries, i.e. $(u_A^N, u_B^N) = (16, 16)$, is a unique Nash and subgame perfect equilibrium. The tax rate is so low that it pays for a country to nationalize irrespective of the behaviour of the other country. Both maximize utility by playing mixed strategies.

In case (ii), both countries play pure strategies, i.e. $(u_A, u_B) = (0, 0)$, which is a unique Nash as well as subgame perfect equilibrium. Since $- 10 < 0$, i.,e. $u^{Na} < u$, it does not pay for one of the countries to nationalize when the other does not. Moreover, because $14 > 4$, i.e. $u^a > u^N$, it does not pay for one of the countries to nationalize when nationalize when the other does. We have here a standard prisoner's dilemma situation. Although the countries together earn most when both play mixed strategies, nobody does in equilibrium.

In case (iii) the two countries are asymmetrical, with nationalization rendering a higher benefit in country B. Because we have $6 > 0$, i.e. $u_B^{Na} > u_B$, but $-10 < 0$, i.e. $u_A^{Na} < u_A$, it pays for country B, but not for country A, to nationalize when the other country does not. Since $4 < 14$, i.e. $u_A^N < u_A^a$, it does not pay for country A to nationalize when country B does. Thus, the outcome $(u_A^a, u_B^{Na}) = (14, 6)$ is a unique Nash as well as subgame perfect equilibrium. In this case, only one country plays the mixed strategy.

Table 5.4 summarizes the three equilibria demonstrated, as well as a fourth possible equilibrium, together with the pay-off relations on which they depend. The pay-off relations refer to whether it pays to play the mixed strategy when the other country does (left hand column) or does not (right hand column) do so. The mixed strategy equilibrium is referred to as 'nationalization' and the pure strategy as 'no nationalization'. In the three cases we have demonstrated, there is a unique Nash equilibrium as well as a subgame perfect equilibrium. In case 1 both countries nationalize, in case 2 neither does and in case 3 only one country nationalizes.

Table 5.4 Unique equilibria in a two-country set-up

Kind of equilibrium	Pay-off relations	Example
1 A nationalize, B nationalize, unique Nash and subgame perfect	$u^N > u^a$, $u^{Na} > u$	(i)
2 No nationalize, unique Nash and subgame perfect	$u^a > u^N$, $u > u^{Na}$	(ii)
3 A not nationalize, B nationalize, unique Nash and subgame perfect	$u^a > u^N$, $u^{Na} > u$	(iii)
4 A nationalize, B nationalize, unique subgame perfect	$u^N > u^a$, $u > u^{Na}$	

With the pay-off relations given in the fourth example, there are two Nash equilibria: nationalization in both countries as well as nationalization in neither country. However, the latter is not subgame perfect, because it hinges on the incredible threat that a country would not follow if one country nationalized. Thus, nationalization in both countries is a unique subgame perfect equilibrium in case 4. This was not illustrated above, because no parameter values in our set-up allow $u^N > u^a$ and $u > u^{Na}$ to be fulfilled at the same time. It still deserves attention, since the correspondence may matter when there are many competing countries, which is relevant for the empirical analyses in the following chapters.

Consider the degree of substitutability between the two countries in the different equilibria. The closer substitutes the two countries are, the larger the relocation of projects that follows from differing levels of nationalization. As can be checked in Table 5.4, in case 1 the two countries are sufficiently distant substitutes to make it pay to nationalize alone as well as to nationalize if the other country does. Conversely, in case 2 the two countries are sufficiently close substitutes not to allow it to pay to nationalize alone, and make it preferable not to follow when the other country nationalizes. For case 3, however, it pays for one country to nationalize alone but not for the other to follow. This requires that the two countries are sufficiently close substitutes to make it pay to abstain from nationalizing when the other country acts, but distant enough to make it preferable to nationalize when the other country abstains from doing so. Likewise, in case 4 the countries must be sufficiently close substitutes not to make it pay for a country to nationalize alone, but sufficiently distant to make it pay to follow if another country nationalizes.

The third equilibrium in which one country nationalizes, may have various properties. If the third example given above is adjusted so that $u_A^{Na} > u_A$, both countries are better off if they nationalize alone than they are in the case when neither country nationalizes. If, in addition, $u_A^{Na} > u_A^a$ and $u_B^{Na} > u_B^a$, both have an incentive to speed in order to play the mixed strategy first. If, instead, $u_A^{Na} < u_A^a < u_A^a$ and $u_B^{Na} < u_B^a$, both countries have an incentive to wait as long as possible, since it is better to be the country that does not nationalize. Under these circumstances it may be indeterminate which country acts. It could be expected, of course, that the most urgent (least patient) country, probably the one which has the most to gain, acts the fastest or is the most patient.

As mentioned, 1 and 2 are the only possible equilibria when the countries are symmetrical. This is because $u^{Na} > u^N - u^a$ must hold in that case.[8] Since $u = 0$ and u^{Na} is the only pay-off which can be negative, it is seen from Table 5.4 that 3 and 4 cannot occur under these circumstances. With symmetrical countries, we have either an equilibrium in which both nationalize or one in which neither country does. This does not rule out equilibria 3 or 4, since the real world is undoubtedly characterized by asymmetrical countries. Nevertheless, these equilibria can be expected to be less plausible than the first two, as seen from the conflicting properties in terms of substitutability which pertain to them.

It can be argued that, in practice, host countries are likely to have some information on the profitability of individual investment projects. In this case, nationalization should not be pursued completely at random. Firms that do well and/or can be effectively run under domestic ownership would be particularly susceptible to takeover. This increases the disincentive effect on direct investment, because firms sense that they suffer a greater risk of being nationalized when they do well. Accordingly, the motivation for undertaking direct investment is then reduced. In the extreme case of complete information, the firms that it would pay to nationalize are discouraged from investing in the first place, and no nationalization will be observed. As long as we do not have complete information on the part of host countries, our results remain valid.

To sum up, in this section we have demonstrated the existence of two plausible equilibria which are unique for given parameter values when countries are symmetrical: in one, both countries nationalize selectively; in the other, neither of them nationalizes. An alternative equilibrium, in which only one country nationalizes selectively, hinges on asymmetry between the two countries and is argued to be less plausible. In the next section we discuss which factors determine equilibria or may cause shifts between them.

DETERMINANTS OF NATIONALIZATION

Consider Table 5.5 which summarizes the conditions which are crucial for determining subgame perfect equilibria in the two-country framework. If both $u^N > u^a$ and $u^{Na} > u$ are fufilled, it is a unique Nash equilibrium as well as a subgame perfect equilibrium that both countries play the mixed strategy with selective nationalization. If $u^N > u^a$ is fulfilled, but not $u^{Na} > u$, nationalization in both countries is not a unique Nash equilibrium but is still a unique subgame perfect equilibrium. If $u^{Na} > u$ is fulfilled, but not $u^N > u^a$, one country nationalizes and one does not. For no country to nationalize it is required that both $u^{Na} < u$ and $u^N < u^a$ hold.

Table 5.5 Conditions for two-country subgame perfect equilibria

Pay-off relations	Condition for outcome
$u^N > u^a$	Sufficient condition for both countries to nationalize
$u^{Na} > u$	Sufficient condition for one country to nationalize
$u^{Na} < u$	Necessary condition for no nationalization
$u^N < u^a$	Necessary condition for no nationalization

The condition $u^{Na} > u$ for nationalization in one country is normally fulfilled when $u^N > u^a$. With symmetrical countries, this is always the case. Thus, we can view $u^N > u^a$, the sufficient condition for nationalization in both countries, as crucial for the occurrence of the policy. This choice is supported in the next chapter, in which the analysis is generalized to a framework of many countries. We argue that nationalization hinges on whether it pays for a country to nationalize when its competitor does, rather than whether it pays for a country to nationalize on its own. If this proposition is correct, it explains why it has not been possible to understand variations in nationalization by looking solely at the costs or benefits which prevail for individual countries.

The determinants of the condition $u^N > u^a$ may vary, but the following four factors should play a role, with an impact as indicated:

- The ratio π/π^N of the profit under foreign ownership to that subsequent to nationalization exerts a negative impact on nationalization.
- The tax rate ϕ, which represents the extent to which a host country gains from direct investment under foreign ownership, exerts a negative impact.
- The sunk cost S exerts a positive impact as long as it is fairly small relative to the profitability of most direct investment. The larger S is, the less investment a country attracts by not nationalizing when the other country does. If S is very large, its impact becomes negative because nationalization in both countries would discourage more or less all investment. We neglect this possibility.
- The substitutability μ of the two countries exerts a negative impact. The larger it is, the more investment a country attracts by not nationalizing when its rival does.

Two additional factors may be of interest. First, the variation in the level of profits between firms exerts a negative impact if the amount of direct investment discouraged, or attracted by a country which does not nationalize, increases. On the other hand, there is a positive impact if host countries have some information on which firms have higher profits and can thereby increase the benefits from nationalization. Because its influence is ambiguous, this factor is omitted. Second, the discount factor δ exerts a negative impact on nationalization when future direct investment is discouraged. This is the case if there is some room for countries to nationalize by surprise, which is possible when, for example, MNEs estimate the risk of nationalization partly on the basis of a country's past behaviour. As nationalization is or is not pursued, a reputation effect makes firms view a country as more or less inclined to nationalize.[9]

On this basis, we can formulate the following hypothesis regarding what factors determine whether nationalization occurs in two competing countries:

$$N = \psi \quad (\delta, \quad \pi/\pi^N, \quad \phi, \quad S, \quad \mu) \quad (5.11)$$
$$ (-) \quad (-) \qquad (-) \quad (+) \quad (-)$$

which states that nationalization is more likely the smaller the discount factor, the greater the rents that can be captured under domestic ownership relative to the profit under foreign (the smaller the direct cost), the lower the tax rate, the larger the sunk cost and the less the two countries are substitutes for direct investment. The last two factors represent different aspects of the 'mobility' of investment projects. The more mobile projects are, in the sense that the sunk cost is small or the level of profit in two competing countries is similar, the lower the probability that nationalization pays.

These factors can be interpreted as indicating which developments may cause a shift from an equilibrium with nationalization to one without, or vice versa. Expression (5.11) suggests that nationalization may be started (brought to an end) by the following factors: a decline (increase) in the discount factor, perhaps brought about by an increase (reduction) in the international interest rate; an increase (reduction) in the profits that can be captured under domestic ownership, possibly attributable to an increase (fall) in export prices or a greater (lesser) ability on the part of a host country to run a subsidiary on its own; a decline (increase) in tax rates; an increased (reduced) 'sunkenness' of investment; a wider (narrower) profit differential between competing host countries.

It should be noted that greater effects are required to prevent nationalization to the extent that host countries co-operate rather than compete. In our framework, it can be said that the occurrence of nationalization is interpreted in terms of a co-ordination problem. Given strategic complementarities, meaning that an increase in one player's strategy increases the optimal strategy of another player, it is well known that co-ordination problems may give rise to multiple equilibria, and that these may be inefficient (Cooper and John 1988).

Is there a *raison d'être* to step in and prevent nationalization in the event that the policy pays? Again, the answer is 'yes', since some direct investment is discouraged and potential mutual profits are therefore forgone. In the case when nationalization is pursued in both countries, some direct investment is discouraged in both of them. In the event that countries adopt different degrees of nationalization, some projects are also relocated from where they can generate the greatest profits to where the profits are smaller, which involves an efficiency loss. If the absence of nationalization for some reason represents an undesirable distribution of gains between MNEs and host countries, the distribution should be adjusted by other measures which do not discourage undertaking direct investment. Once again, the fact that nationalization is not observed need not mean that the policy does not play a role. This matter is returned to in Chapter 7.

There may be varying opinions on which measures are the most appropriate to rule out the risk of nationalization. In principle, it could be achieved through any of the factors given in (5.11). For example, a higher discount factor could be induced, tax rates could be raised or stiffer host country competition could be stimulated until the equilibrium without nationalization would be assured. Of course, different measures affect the distribution of gains from direct investment differently, which must be taken into account.

SUMMARY AND CONCLUSIONS

The benefits of nationalization can be assumed to derive from the retention of profits which cannot be taxed. Given complete information, rational firms do not invest in the first place if they are to be nationalized. With incomplete information and an infinite time horizon, MNEs may pursue a strategy where they do not invest in a country that has nationalized. In theory, such trigger strategy equilibria have been shown to prevent nationalization altogether. In practice, however, MNEs do not formulate strategies collectively, and nationalization does occur at times.

In this chapter we have considered that host countries may play mixed strategies, nationalizing firms selectively on a random basis. A country is assumed to ruin its reputation only when a continuation of its present policy would reduce the expected profits of firms below zero. For a single country in which firms earn the same profit, there is a unique mixed strategy equilibrium that comprises the greatest amount of selective nationalization that does not reduce firms' expected profit below zero, and which is therefore compatible with the undertaking of direct investment. However, the greater the share which is nationalized in equilibrium, the higher are the pre-tax profits required to cover the risk for firms to be nationalized. Thus, the risk of nationalization discourages some direct investment from being undertaken.

The extent to which nationalization discourages direct investment is determined by the opportunity costs of firms, which are in turn determined by the availability of alternative investment locations. This is influenced by the behaviour of other potential host countries, which raises the issue of co-ordination problems between countries. To study nationalization in host countries which compete for gains from direct investment, we introduced a two-country framework. The countries simply face a dichotomous choice: whether to play a mixed strategy with a certain 'optimal level' of selective national-ization or a pure strategy without any nationalization. Profits vary among projects according to a uniform distribution, and are more or less independent in the two countries. The countries are aware of the distribution, but have incomplete information on the profitability of specific projects.

In this framework, we have demonstrated two subgame perfect equilibria, unique for given parameter specifications. In the first, both countries nationalize selectively; in the second, neither country nationalizes. We argue that the crucial condition is whether it pays for a country to follow when the other one acts. It is suggested that nationalizations may start (terminate) owing to a decline (increase) in the discount factor, an increased (reduced) profit under domestic ownership relative to foreign ownership, a decline (increase) in tax rates, an increased (reduced) 'sunkenness' of investment or a wider (narrower) profit differential between competing host countries.

The condition for nationalization amounts to a requirement that two countries are sufficiently distant substitutes for direct investment, and the condition for no nationalization is that they are sufficiently close substitutes. If import-substituting direct investment is characterized by less substitutability than export-oriented investment, nationalization is more probable when there is a great deal of the former. It should be noted that Chapter 3 indicated a lower tax rate, the greater the degree of substitutability between host countries, which should increase the probability that nationalization pays. Clarifying these counteracting influences when both policies adapt simultaneously may be an interesting topic for future research.

In contrast with taxation, the possibility of nationalization may discourage some direct investment, and possibly distort its pattern across countries. From the point of overall welfare there is consequently a poten-tial *raison d'être* for preventing nationalization. In principle this can be achieved through any of the factors mentioned above. if the distribution of gains between MNEs and host countries is considered to be socially suboptimal, this should be adjusted for by other means than nationalization.

In Chapters 3 and 5 we have developed models of taxation and nationalization of MNE affiliates when potential host countries compete for gains from direct investment. The model results obtained form a conceptual basis and a starting point for an empirically relevant analysis. For example, in Chapter 4 we applied the findings on taxation to pollution intensive direct investment. As taxation refers to the total burden of policies that target the behaviour of MNEs, however, it is difficult to obtain consistent cross-country data on this policy. In the next chapter we turn to empirical tests of the nationalization policy.

6 Cross-country variation in nationalization

INTRODUCTION

As concluded in Chapter 1, the state which emerged in the international arena in the late 1960s has been characterized by sovereign nations subject to a lack of strict rules. Our working assumption is that host country behaviour from that time can be understood as motivated by socio-economic goals. This may seem a bold assumption, but its applicability in the present context has gained support from a number of studies. Concerning the period when selective nationalizations peaked, Kobrin (1980, 1984), Jodice (1980) and Minor (1988) have demonstrated the importance of economic factors. The last of these studies also refuted previous allegations that political factors would have exerted a significant impact on the cross-country pattern of nationalization.

Despite the studies mentioned, there is still no satisfactory explanation of why and when countries actually pursue nationalization. The findings regarding the particular country characteristics that spurred nationalization in the 1970s do not apply to the 1980s, when there has been almost no nationalization. To help fill the gap, this and the following chapter build on the notion developed in Chapter 5, namely that the nationalization behaviour of potential host countries which compete for gains from direct investment is interdependent.[1]

In this chapter, we are concerned with the cross-country variation in nationalization over the period when the policy peaked, i.e. 1968–79. First we survey the empirical record and point out weaknesses in some previous work. Our theoretical framework is presented next, and the data base is introduced in the following section. We then discuss hypotheses and variables for empirical testing. A country's decision whether or not to nationalize at all during the period 1968–79 is explained by a probit model, and the results of the probit test are presented. The variation in the number of years of nationalization is explained within the framework of a count data binomial regression model. For its estimation, a semiparametric estimator is extended to this model type. The results of the binomial regression are analysed in the penultimate section, and the chapter is summarized in the final section. The results should be contrasted with those in Chapter 7, in which the termination of nationalization in the late 1970s is examined.

THE EMPIRICAL RECORD

The unit of study in this and the following chapter is a so-called act of nationalization, which involves the takeover of any number of firms in a single industry in a given year. Figure 6.1 illustrates the cross-time distribution of acts between 1960 and 1985, divided into four regions: the Middle East, Latin America, Asia and Africa (the latter two exclude the Middle East). Figure 6.2 illustrates the cross-time distribution by sectors: natural resources, manufacturing, agriculture, banking and insurance, and others.[2] Figure 6.3 shows the number of countries acting each year by regions.

The total number of acts was fairly stable until the late 1960s. Exceptions were 1959 (not included in the figures), 1964–5 and 1967. The peaks in these years partly stemmed from acts undertaken in Cuba, Indonesia and Tanzania at these times. In the late 1960s there was a sharp increase in nationalization, up to 53 acts per year on average in the first half of the 1970s. Figure 6.1 shows that the increase occurred across the Middle East, Latin America and Africa. Asia had a minor peak solely in 1964–5. Moreover, the number of countries that nationalized rose from ten or less each year before 1969 to a level of twenty to thirty. This increase took place mainly in Latin America and Africa, while the Middle East experienced a peak between 1972 and 1974. According to Kobrin (1980), 4.4 per cent of the stock of partially or wholly foreign-owned firms in developing countries at year end 1976, plus the expropriations, were taken over between 1968 and 1976. Jodice (1980) estimated that 12 per cent of the stock of direct investment in developing countries in 1967 was nationalized up to 1976. There was extensive nationalization during these years, but it was still modest relative to the total stock of direct investment.

It should be recalled from Chapter 1 that nationalization was held back by the threat of retaliatory home country action up to the late 1960s. Most acts so far were of a 'mass' character, and primarily politically/ ideologically motivated.[3] From the late 1960s, however, there was a rapid increase in selective nationalization, which was pursued independently of the ideological orientation of host countries. These acts

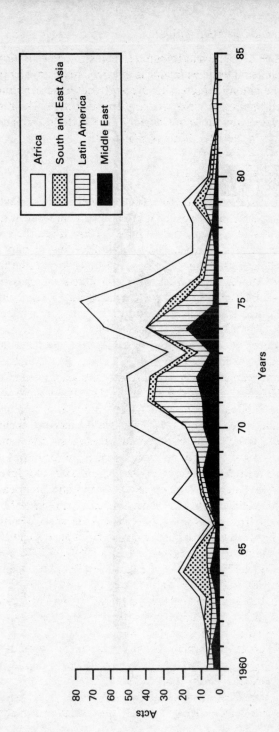

Figure 6.1 The cross-time distribution of nationalization across regions

Sources: Kobrin 1986; Minor 1987

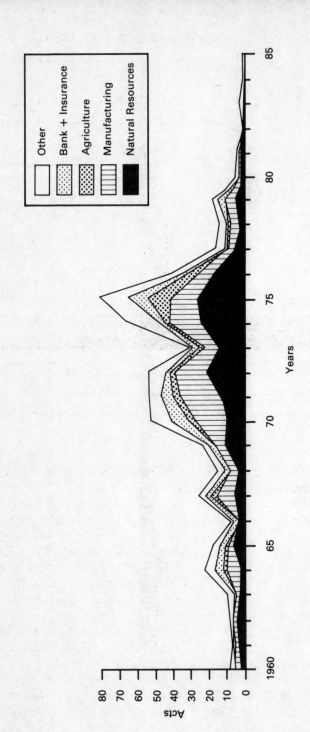

Figure 6.2 The cross-time distribution of nationalization across sectors
Sources: Kobrin 1986; Minor 1987

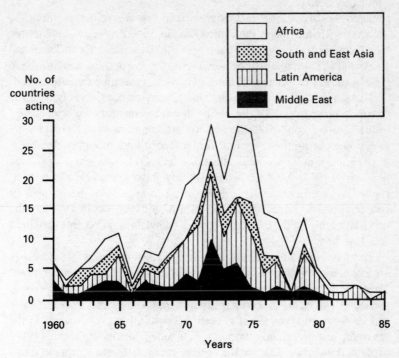

Figure 6.3 The number of countries undertaking nationalization across regions
Sources: Kobrin 1986; Minor 1987

were relatively inconspicuous, and were often accompanied by encouragement to obtain new investment.

From the 1960s, nationalization has been associated with industry and project-related factors. Kobrin (1980) found that sectoral belonging, ownership technology, level and maturity of technology and home country belonging influence the propensity of certain activities to be nationalized. The sectoral distribution 1960–79 was as follows: natural resources, 31 per cent; manufacturing, 27 per cent; agriculture, 9 per cent; banking and insurance, 12 per cent; others, 21 per cent.[4] Drawing a comparison with the number of firms in the period 1960–76, natural resources, infrastructure and banking and insurance had the highest propensity to be nationalized. Manufacturing and trade were relatively less vulnerable. Meanwhile, wholly owned subsidiaries were the target of some 75 per cent of all acts. Investment that had reached a mature phase of its life cycle, possessed a technology that was easy to copy and had developed local management was highly susceptible to takeover. Investment that originated in responsive home countries, such as the United States, the United Kingdom and France, was somewhat more secure on average. In a more general discussion, De la Torre and Neckar (1988) distinguish between industry, corporate, structural and managerial factors as determinants of activities that may be nationalized.

The number of nationalizations has fluctuated considerably over the years. It turned out that the 1968–76 phase constituted a spectacular peak. 72.1 per cent of all the acts undertaken between 1960 and 1985 took place during these years. From a record high of eighty-three acts in 1975, the number of nationalizations declined to an average of sixteen per year in 1977–9, which is only slightly above the level before 1968. Figure 6.3 confirms that the downturn also applied to the number of countries acting, although there was a minor increase in 1979. In the first half of the 1980s, the occurrence of nationalization became stabilized at a low level.

The downturn in nationalization is analysed in Chapter 7. Here, we are concerned with cross-country variations in the policy at its peak. There have been a great many empirical studies of nationalization, particularly in business administration. Based on the experiences of Zaire and Zambia, Shafer (1985) related the costs of nationalization to the strength, resources and autonomy of a state. Burton and Inoue (1984) explained the occurrence of the policy among different sectors in terms of a country's stage of economic development. Juhl (1985) supported the view that nationalization increases with a country's capacity to assume responsibility for an affiliate. Here, we focus on the work of Jodice (1980) who explained some 60 per cent of the cross-country variation in natural resource nationalization in the period 1968–76 by combining socio-economic and political explanatory variables in a multiple regression model. The following explanatory variables were reported as significant:

1   the level of modernity of a country (measured by gross national product per capita (GNP/c)), which exerts a curvilinear effect;
2   government capacity (measured by the ratio of central government revenue to GDP);
3   economic performance failure (measured by instability of export earnings);
4   lack of government dependence on bilateral aid from the United States;
5   'collective protest' and 'internal war' in a country, indicating political threat directed against the government with respect to its ability to withstand such pressure.

The first two variables would reflect the ability of host countries to run nationalized subsidiaries on their own. The propensity to nationalize would increase with the level of economic development and administrative capacity of a country. However, the most developed countries would already have nationalized their natural resources in 1967, causing the curvilinear effect. Policy failure matters, according to Jodice, because 'nationalization is rooted in the frustration of politicians'. The fourth variable is a disincentive since dependence on US aid makes countries vulnerable to sanctions from the major, as well as most responsive, home country. The fifth variable indicates domestic pressure to take forceful action against MNEs. Where authorities have difficulty in handling domestic opposition, nationalization is useful as a way of demonstrating power of action.

Jodice argued that nationalizations occur because weak regimes capable of running nationalized firms need scapegoats in times of crisis. The influence of the political variable has been questioned because others have been unable to replicate his result. Minor (1988) found no significant impact from this variable, and concluded that 'there is no simple relationship between political threat or instability and the propensity to nationalize'. Political factors are therefore excluded here, although there are examples of selective nationalization where it did play a role.

Jodice's study is generally regarded as one of the most successful in the field. However, it does not explain the variations in nationalization outside natural resources or the period with which he was concerned. The downturn after 1976 cannot be explained by, for example, 'less policy failure'. It could, of course, be argued that all possible targets had been taken at the time. However, this is doubtful given real world observations of what investment remains. Moreover, the time pattern of nationalization in natural resources does not deviate much from that in other sectors, in which the cessation of the policy is even less capable of explanation by the above factors. We do not yet have a clear picture of when and why nationalization can be expected to occur.

THEORETICAL FRAMEWORK

It was demonstrated in Chapter 5 that, when two countries compete for gains from direct investment, the amount discouraged by nationalization depends on the behaviour of both of them. If one country nationalizes alone, it discourages more investment than if both nationalize, as it then loses investment projects to the other. Two plausible equilibria, unique for given parameter values, were demonstrated, one in which nationalization pays in both countries and one in which it does not pay in either of them. It was argued that the crucial condition for which equilibrium prevails was whether or not it pays to nationalize when the other country does.

Again, nationalization is mainly a measure to prevent repatriation of profits, which suggests that the objective is short-term foreign exchange earnings. The gain has to be weighed against losses which are primarily of a long-run character. A loss of firm-specific advantages which are inherent to the parent company, and possibly a discouragement of future undertaking of direct investment, means that capital, technology, employment, risk-diversification etc. are foregone by the host country. To the extent that nationalization is considered at all, there should be a trade-off between capturing short-term gains and suffering relatively long-term losses.[5]

The two-country analysis can be generalized to a framework of many potential host countries which compete for gains from direct investment. The following condition for a firm undertaking direct investment in country i was given in Chapter 2:

$$
\begin{aligned}
f \text{ in } i \text{ iff: } & E[(1 - \phi_i)\pi_i - \Phi_i] (1 - r_i) - S_i] \geqslant \\
& \max (E\{[(1 - \phi_j)\pi_j - \Phi_j] (1 - r_j) - S_j\},0) \\
& \qquad j \neq i
\end{aligned}
\tag{6.1}
$$

which says that the firm f sets up a subsidiary in country i if and only if its expected rate of return is positive and higher than it is in the best alternative host country j. π is the pre-tax profit, ϕ is the corporate income tax, Φ is a lump-sum tax, r is the estimated risk of nationalization and S is the sunk cost required for investment. Host countries, on the other hand, must consider whether investors pull out or abstain from investing in the future in case they nationalize. The policy pays provided that the benefits outweigh the direct and indirect costs. The maximization problem for country i, again restated from Chapter 2, can be written

$$
\begin{aligned}
\max_{\phi,\Phi,\lambda} \quad & \sum_{t=1}^{\infty} \sum_{f=1}^{n_t} \quad [(1 - \lambda_f)(\phi_{ft}\pi_{ft} + \Phi_{ft} + X_{Gft} - X_{Bft}) \\
& + \lambda_f(\pi_{ft}^{N} + X_{Gft}^{N} - X_{Bft}^{N})
\end{aligned}
$$

subject to f in i, $\phi_f \epsilon [0, 1]$ and $\lambda_f \epsilon \{0, 1\}$ $\tag{6.2}$

where X_G and X_B are the values of positive and negative external effects, and superscript N marks profits and external effects subsequent to nationalization. Again, (6.2) states that country i maximizes its utility over an infinite time horizon and a potential flow of n investment projects each period. Gains accrue from each project through nationalization or taxation, as well as from external effects, subject to the constraint that projects are undertaken, which is expression (6.1) for each MNE.

How much direct investment is discouraged by nationalization depends on the availability of alternative investment opportunities. Since each project is characterized by firm-specific advantages, countries are likely to be differentially close substitutes for different projects. From the perspective of an individual country, the behaviour of all competing countries is more or less relevant. Generally speaking, the greater the number of competing countries that nationalize as well, the smaller is the discouraging effect on direct investment and the smaller is the captured rent which makes nationalization pay. The fewer competing countries that nationalize, the larger is the discouraging effect and the larger is the captured rent required for the policy to pay.

Against this background, two extreme 'global' equilibria may be considered, one in which all countries nationalize selectively and one in which none do. In the first, it pays to nationalize because others do as well. MNEs perceive no great differences in the risk of being nationalized in different locations, and the policy consequently causes relatively little discouragement of direct investment from the individual countries. The firms that abstain from direct investment in a country, because of the risk of being nationalized, are those that abstain in developing countries altogether. In the second equilibrium, it does not pay for individual countries to nationalize, because others would not follow if they did and they would lose direct investment to their competitors.

Between the extremes, there may be intermediate stages in which not all countries act one way or the other. With more than two countries, there are certain to be asymmetries between individual countries and their competitors. Moreover, since countries are differentially close substitutes for investment projects, there may be groups which do or do not nationalize depending on the behaviour of their closest competitors. There may also be individual outliers due to extreme costs or benefits, or political motives. Thus, co-operation problems between the many developing countries that compete for gains from direct investment may give rise to an unknown number of multiple equilibria in the occurrence of nationalization.

The disincentive effect of being one of a few which pursue nationalization is likely to be pronounced, because most projects will have fairly similar alternative locations where they do not face the risk of being nationalized. The gain of being one of a few countries which abstain from nationalization may be less pronounced, however, since a particular country is a suitable host for a limited number of projects. Consequently, it is unlikely that it pays for a country to nationalize alone, which supports the argument that the crucial condition for nationalization is whether it pays for other countries to follow when an individual country acts. In a state where nationalization is largely absent, the reason is not primarily that it does not pay for individual countries, but rather that it would not pay for others to follow if a country acted. If others were to follow, nationalization would pay and the policy would be enacted on a large scale. The implication is that small exogenous changes may set off nationalization across a large number of countries.

In the opposite situation, where nationalization is pursued by many countries, the policy would be discontinued if it paid for some to stop when others acted. However, the incentive for an individual country to initiate the halt may be weak for the reason given above. Thus, it seems plausible that the termination of selective nationalization requires other factors, apart from the discouragement of direct investment, such as a depressed stock of investment projects that can be taken, increased economic retaliation by home countries or international organizations, discouragement of portfolio investment etc. We return to these issues in Chapter 7.

This view of nationalization as influenced by co-ordination problems seems in line with the historical record, although the extreme states of all or no countries acting at a time have not been observed. Only a few countries nationalized each year up to the late 1960s, and in the 1980s. Furthermore, as discussed in Chapter 1, most nationalization up to the late 1960s was of a mass character and hence mainly politically motivated. In the 1980s, the distinction between 'mass' and 'selective' nationalization as defined by Kobrin (1984) cannot be made. However, a look at the countries that acted suggests that political motives did play an important role in this period.[6] Thus, economically motivated nationalization has been even more concentrated than appears from the distribution of the total number of acts shown in Figures 6.1 and 6.2. In the period 1968–79, nationalization was pursued by a majority of the developing countries. The period examined by Jodice (1980) falls within this interval. In the following we seek to explain the cross-country variation in nationalization during the 'peak' of the policy.

DATA

It is difficult to obtain consistent data on nationalization. Rather than developing a new data base, we use the most comprehensive, if not the most extensive, available. This is based on a systematic scanning of secondary sources by Kobrin for the period 1960–79 and Minor (1987) for the subsequent years up to 1985. Nationalization is used as a term for the seizure of equity, and concerns only direct investment – debt repudiation is a more suitable term in the case of portfolio investment. The divestment must be involuntary and cause the deprivation of ownership *per se*. Four types are included: formal expropriation, intervention, forced sale and contract renegotiation leading to transfer of ownership.

The data base includes a total of 574 acts, encompassing about 1,550 individual firms. While most nationalization from 1960 is included, some categories may be under-represented, notably forced sales. Burton and Inoue (1984) examined an even larger data base, consisting of 1,857 cases, including for the first time Japanese firms. However, their data are less comprehensive in some respects, and are not as up to date as those used here.

The seriousness of nationalization in the eyes of investors depends on the proportion of foreign-owned assets which is taken, the amount of compensation and the practice of negotiation. Unfortunately, these factors are impossible to observe or quantify in any detail. Likewise, the number of acts or firms taken, which have been used in some previous tests, are inadequate proxies for the amount of nationalization. Thus, it is difficult to test explanations of the value, intensity or extension of the policy. Instead, we undertake two model-based tests of whether countries nationalize at all. A related test follows in Chapter 7.

The sample tested here includes sixty-seven observations (countries), which are all developing countries with a stock of direct investment of at least $60 million on average in the period 1972–4 according to UNCTC (1983). Three countries with missing values in one variable had to be excluded, reducing the number of observations to sixty-four.[7] The lower limit is used to avoid inclusion of countries where nationalization was ruled out because of a lack of targets. Together the countries excluded were hosts to less than 2 per cent of the total stock of direct investment in developing countries.[8]

Since the data report acts of nationalization each year in each country it is possible to use corresponding observations of explanatory variables. This type of panel data enables more powerful tests of structural shifts and dependence between observations to be carried out (see Andersson and Brännäs 1990b). There are difficulties, however. First, it is far from certain how agents form their expectations concerning the future. To what extent do they extrapolate past trends and to what extent do they foresee future changes? Second, the requirement of yearly data prevents inclusion of some countries for which data cannot be obtained. Tests based on a single set-up of explanatory variables are less dependent on the dynamic model specification. We use values for individual years for variables which remained at a fairly stable level, and we make estimates roughly corresponding to the average of the period studied for the others.

HYPOTHESES AND VARIABLES

We have suggested that nationalization is motivated by large outflows of foreign exchange which can be prevented through this policy, and by a great need on the part of a host country to nationalize. The larger the rent that can be withheld through nationalization in comparison with taxation, and the higher the opportunity cost for foreign exchange, the greater are the potential benefits of nationalization. Here, we expect characteristics associated with these benefits to exert a significant influence on the cross-country variation in the policy. Because most countries nationalized in the period dealt with, we do not expect a decisive influence to be exerted by factors related to the indirect effects of discouraging direct investment. However, there may still be some effects of that kind. These would be the more pronounced the closer the substitution between countries that did and did not nationalize.

Two tests are undertaken in the following. First, if any nationalization destroys a country's reputation, we should focus on the dichotomous choice as to whether a country nationalizes at all. The question is whether the net value of a great many factors pushed the net benefit of nationalization above zero at any time. A probit model is used for the analysis. Second, nationalization may exert a marginal impact on a country's reputation. Given that a reputation can be restored – that past acts become less important as long as a country does not act anew – the policy's frequency in time should matter. Every time a country acts anew, this signals a danger of continuation. When it does not act, it signals that there is less danger of continuation. Based on this conception, we use a binomial regression model to explain cross-country variation in the frequency of the policy.

The dependent variables are as follows: in the probit model, a dichotomous variable taking a value of zero if a country did not nationalize in the period 1968–79, and otherwise unity; in the binomial regression model, the number of years in the period 1968–79 in which countries undertook at least one act of nationalization, indicating how often they inflicted the indirect costs on themselves.

Concerning explanatory variables, the factors given in (5.11) are not directly observable. Instead, we have chosen acceptable proxy variables with a view to the goal of being able to include as many countries as possible in the testing. The definitions of the explanatory variables and descriptive statistics are given in Table 6.1. The rationale for their inclusion, and the expected impact, is described below for each variable.

Table 6.1 Definitions of variables and descriptive statistics

Definition of variable		Mean	Median	Standard deviation	n
X_1	Direct investment (stock, 1974)	778	340	1,337	67
X_2	Average growth (1970–9)	4.3	4.5	3.1	67
X_3	GDP (1974)	12,684	3,528	22,524	67
X_4	GDP/c (1979)	1,553	740	2,523	67
X_5	Export commodity concentration (%)	39.8	36.1	26.6	64
X_{5D}	Export commodity concentration (low/high)	0.25	0	0.44	64

X_1, the stock of direct investment, is the prime indicator of the indirect effect of discouraging direct investment. The greater the stock, the greater is the amount of direct investment that may be pulled out of a country. In particular, the size of the stock indicates the potential for reinvestment as well as repatriation of profits which may occur in response to the policy. Thus, we expect a significant negative impact on nationalization if the disincentive effect is of great importance. However, the variable may also indicate the availability of suitable targets. If this effect dominates, we expect a positive impact.

X_2, the growth rate, is a proxy variable for an economy's 'soundness', or economic performance. First, it is negatively related to the opportunity cost of foreign exchange. High growth should make foreign creditors more willing to provide lending, should make foreign as well as domestic firms less inclined to capital flight, should provide better prospects for export earnings and so forth. Second, growth should enhance the attractiveness of taxation, because the host country is a more desirable location for future activities and foreign investors are therefore more inclined to reinvest than to repatriate profits excessively. Thus, we expect a negative impact on nationalization.[9]

X_3, the size of the economy (GDP), is a proxy variable for capital mobility between a country and the rest of the world, i.e. the sensitivity of investment flows with respect to host country action (cf. Huizinga 1988). The larger the economy, the less easily is direct investment discouraged by nationalization. Thus, if the discouraging effect is important, we expect a significant positive impact of GDP on nationalization.

On the other hand, the size of the economy should be positively related to the tax rate (as this increases with low capital mobility), which suggests a negative impact on nationalization.

X_4, the income level (GDP/c), indicates the level of sophistication in the host economy, including the quality of its infrastructure. Because this is related to a country's ability to attract direct investment, there should be a negative impact on nationalization to the extent that the disincentive effect exerts a major impact. It is true that the income level indicates a country's capacity to run nationalized firms on its own. This is the argument made by Jodice (1980) for a positive impact on a country's propensity to nationalize. As put forward by Bergsten et al. (1978), however, higher income also raises a country's ability to earn from investment under foreign ownership.

X_5, the export commodity concentration, indicates the vulnerability of a country's external position. A positive impact is expected because a high concentration is likely to induce a great need for short-term foreign exchange earnings in response to fluctuations in, for example, commodity prices. Two alternative measures are used: first, the highest value recorded for the share of fuels, minerals and metals as a percentage of total merchandise exports in 1970 and 1980; second, a dummy variable X_{5D} which takes a value of unity if this share surpassed 80 per cent in either of those years, and otherwise is zero. The dummy is motivated by a high concentration being likely to exert an impact, while variation at a low level should not matter.

Summing up, we expect the cross-country variation in nationalization in the period 1968–79 to be determined by the rate of growth and the export commodity concentration, because these variables should be respectively negatively and positively related to the potential benefits of nationalization. The other variables are argued to be associated primarily with the indirect effects from discouraging direct investment, which should be relatively unimportant for explaining cross-country variation in nationalization in the period studied.

THE PROBIT MODEL

Consider a dichotomous choice model where a country either does or does not nationalize. Because there may be overt or covert compensation, in certain cases nationalization may not represent acts of forced divestment but may occur with the consent of the MNEs targeted. In order to lessen the risk that such events classify countries as having nationalized when they have not, we require that a country undertook at least two acts of nationalization in the period studied in order to be recorded as having nationalized. Then the country is assigned a value of unity (indicating nationalization).

In the following we give only a brief description of the probit model (for a more thorough discussion, see Amemiya (1981), and for a related model test, see Lall (1986)). Let the expected gain of nationalization be $X\beta_*$, where X is a vector corresponding to the attributes of individual countries and β_* is a vector of unknown parameters. For the ith country, the decision to nationalize is taken if and only if

$$X_i\beta_* + \epsilon_i > 0 \tag{6.3}$$

where $\epsilon_i \sim N(0, \sigma^2)$. The probability that the country nationalizes can be determined from the distribution of ϵ_i and is given by $1 - \phi(-X_i\beta)$, where $\phi(.)$ is the standard normal distribution function. The log likelihood function is maximized with respect to $\beta = \beta_*/\sigma$ through the standard identifying condition. The β can be interpreted as the impact of various country attributes on the probability of nationalizing.

RESULTS OF THE PROBIT MODEL

The estimates obtained using the probit model are given in Table 6.2. The first run includes the commodity concentration variable (in per cent), which is replaced in the second run by the dummy variable X_{5D}. All other variables are included in both runs. In the third run, the dummy construction is retained, and the variable with the smallest t value in the second run (X_1) has been dropped. The logarithmic form has been used for X_1, X_3, X_4 and X_5 in order to restrict the dominating impact of a few very large observations.

Some alternative measures of the explanatory power of a probit model, suggested by Amemiya (1981), are given below the estimates in Table 6.2. The explanatory power increases in the first measure and decreases in the last three. Comparing the first two runs, it can be seen that the dummy construction is superior in all measures except for the Effron R2. The third run is similarly superior to the first.[10] Since we have a good argument for the dummy construction, we pay most attention to the runs based on this. Because all known scalar criteria are subject to weaknesses (cf. Amemiya 1981), we focus on the t values of the explanatory variables in the following.

As can be seen, the stock of direct investment (X_1) has the smallest t value. Moreover, its sign varies, being negative with the commodity concentration in percentage form and positive with the dummy construction. This suggests that the disincentive effect on direct investment did not play a major role. However, GDP (X_3) is significant at the 5 per cent level in the first and third runs and exerts a positive impact as expected with a disincentive effect. GDP/c (X_4) is significant

Table 6.2 Estimation results of the probit model

Variable	β		
	Run 1	*Run 2*	*Run 3*
Intercept	−0.197	0.845	0.643
	(−0.65)	(0.46)	(0.36)
ln X_1	−0.126	0.175	–
	(−0.56)	(0.67)	–
X_2	−0.321	−0.319	−0.327
	(−3.23)	(−2.95)	(−3.07)
ln X_3	0.405	0.339	0.431
	(2.00)	(1.48)	(2.41)
ln X_4	−0.034	−0.461	−0.382
	(−0.16)	(−1.65)	(−1.51)
ln X_5	0.221	–	–
	(1.79)	–	–
X_{5D}	–	2.246	2.067
	–	(2.83)	(2.90)
Effron R^2	0.81	0.48	0.23
No. of wrong predictions (%)	66.6	34.4	42.2
Sum of squared residuals (SSR)	42.0	22.0	26.5
SSR weighted	1.01×10^{13}	2.65×10^{12}	6.67×10^{11}

Note: *t* values in parentheses; size of sample, 64.

at the 10 per cent level in the second run, and exerts a negative impact as expected. The *t* values of these variables are only at the margin of being significant, however, and they are not robust with respect to the model specification. Although there may have been a certain disincentive effect, the results indicate that it was not of primary importance. Before drawing definite conclusions on this point, however, we consider the binomial model.

The rate of growth (X_2) and export commodity concentration (X_{5D}) render inconclusive results. Both exert an impact as expected and are not only significant at the 5 per cent level but have the highest *t* values in all three runs. That the indicators of the effect of discouraging direct investment discussed above did not display any convincing impact suggests that the impacts of both these variables derive from their association with the benefits of nationalization. We could look at marginal effects to obtain more information in the different effects. However, the probit model must be regarded as a fairly crude method in our case. As was made clear, we do not believe that an act of nationalization destroys a country's reputation altogether. We should be able to obtain more reliable results with a binomial regression model.

BINOMIAL MODEL AND ESTIMATION

The use of a probit model for examining cross-country variation in nationalization is not without difficulties. Given that nationalization exerts a gradual and transitory effect on a country's reputation, the policy's frequency in time should matter. In examining cross-country variation in the frequency of nationalization in the period 1968–79, the number of years a country acted is used as the dependent variable. The variable is obviously discrete and ranges from zero to a maximum of 12 years.[11]

We view nationalization in each year as a Bernoulli distributed random variable. Given independence between years, the resulting variable – the number of years of nationalization – is binomially distributed. In a binomial regression model, the probability p of nationalization is typically set equal to a distribution function to guarantee that the estimated probability remains in the permissible range. With a logistic function we have the Bernoulli probabilities of nationalization or non-nationalization in each year in the form of a logit model. With a standard normal distribution function we instead have the probit model. The use of a wider class of distribution functions has been proposed by, for example, Prentice (1975), who suggested the generalized F distribution as a way of reducing the risk of distributional misspecifications.

Here, we adopt the logistic distribution (and supply some empirical support for the specification below), so that the probability of nationalization for the ith country is

$$P_i = \frac{1}{1 + \exp(X\beta)} \tag{6.4}$$

where X is the $(1 \times k)$ vector of explanatory variables and β is the $(k \times 1)$ vector of unknown parameters to be estimated.

The decision to nationalize is not expected to be perfectly independent over the years but, without panel type data, we cannot study this matter in any depth and detail. Moreover, and perhaps because of potential dependence between years, the variance of the number of years of nationalization is not smaller than the mean (cf. Figure 6.4), as it should be with the binomial distribution. Consequently, we propose using a

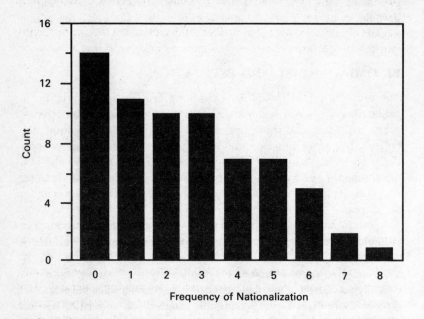

Figure 6.4 The number of years of nationalization: frequencies (mean, 2.63; variance, 4.76; $n = 64$)
Note: To avoid confusion it should be emphasized that 'frequency' refers to the number of years in which a country nationalized, and is not counted over a number of countries.

binomial regression model that takes the 'over-dispersion' or unobserved heterogeneity into account. Over-dispersion can arise as a result of, for example, omitted, proxy or error contaminated variables, or random parameters (cf. Brännäs and Rosenqvist 1988).

Treating the over-dispersion as a random variable θ (with an unknown distribution function) we write the probability $p = 1/[1 + \exp(X\beta + \theta)]$. Dunn *et al.* (1987) suggested a semiparametric estimator for a related type of model. The unknown β parameters and the shape of the unknown continuous distribution function are estimated jointly. The latter is estimated using a discrete distribution function. The Q points of increase are the mass points θ_j, and the increments q_j are probabilities corresponding to each mass point, where $j = 1, ..., Q$. From general theory it is known that the number Q of mass points is finite (Simar 1976; Lindsay 1983a, b; Heckman and Singer 1984). When the model is estimated without a constant term, the mass points can be interpreted as constant terms. It is possible to predict which constant term is the most likely for each country by logistic discrimination (see p.   ).

The density function to be used for estimation is that for the ith country written in the form of a finite mixture model:

$$\text{pr}(y_i) = \sum_{j}^{Q} q_j \begin{pmatrix} 12 \\ y_i \end{pmatrix} \frac{\lambda_{ij}^{12-y_i}}{(1 + \lambda_{ij})^{12}} \tag{6.5}$$

where $\lambda_{ij} = \exp(X\beta + \theta_j)$ and q_j is the probability associated with mass point θ_j. The log likelihood function is

$$l = \sum_{i}^{N} \log \sum_{j}^{Q} q_j \frac{\lambda_{ij}^{12-y_i}}{(1 + \lambda_{ij})^{12}} \tag{6.6}$$

which is maximized with respect to β, the probabilities q_j and the mass points θ_j.

To decide on the number of mass points, Dunn *et al.* (1987), among others, used the informal criterion to add mass points (increase Q) until the estimates of these start to coincide. Instead, we use a theoretically motivated criterion function (cf. Lindsay 1983a, b). Examples of its use in count data models were given by Brännäs and Rosenqvist (1988). As a criterion for the selection of Q, the function

$$D(\theta) = \sum_{i=1}^{N} \frac{\text{pr}(y_i|\theta)}{\text{pr}(y_i)} - N \tag{6.7}$$

is evaluated for all values $\theta \in \Omega$. This function, which has not been used previously in this kind of model, allows us to investigate features in the data which cannot be directly observed, but which help us to understand the way they are structured. The denominator is evaluated at estimates β, θ_j and q_j and $\text{pr}(y_i|\theta)$ at β. Lindsay (1983a, b) provided conditions on the range and potential gaps of Ω. The global maximum of the likelihood function is obtained at the Q for which $D(\theta) \leqslant 0$. The maximizing estimates (β', θ', q', Q) have the property that $D(\theta'_j) = 0$. For other values on θ, $D(\theta) < 0$.

The parameter estimates are obtained by applying the simplex method to the negative of the log likelihood function (6.6).[12] To estimate the value of Q and to ascertain that the solution obtained is indeed a global maximum, the function in (6.7) is evaluated. The associated covariance matrix is calculated using the approximation due to Berndt *et al.* (1974), with Q treated as fixed. The computational work can be performed on a personal computer. The probability that a given country is associated with a particular mass point or constant term j ($j = 1,\ldots,Q$) is obtained by the Bayes rule as

$$\mathrm{pr}(j|y_i) = \frac{q_j\,\mathrm{pr}(y_i|j)}{\mathrm{pr}(y_i)} \tag{6.8}$$

The expression takes the form of a logistic distribution function and is usually called the logistic discriminant function.

RESULTS OF THE BINOMIAL MODEL

The parameter estimates with standard errors are presented in Table 6.3. The t values are obtained by dividing the former by the latter. The two parts of the table correspond to each of the two constructions of

Table 6.3 Estimation results of the binomial model

Variable	X_{5D}	X_5
ln X_1	−0.122 (0.200)	0.045 (0.169)
X_2	0.126 (0.080)	0.212 (0.052)
ln X_3	−0.143 (0.166)	−0.300 (0.153)
ln X_4	0.380 (0.237)	0.185 (0.167)
ln X_5		−0.192 (0.091)
X_{5D}	−1.383 (0.381)	
Constant 1	1.199	3.300
Constant 2	−0.032	2.161
Constant 3	−1.292	0.285
q_1	0.593	0.182
q_2	0.372	0.697
q_3	0.035	0.121
χ^2	98.4	119.7
l	−376.94	−380.88

Note: Standard errors are given in parentheses; the three constants for the semiparametric estimator are mass points of the mixing distribution.

export commodity concentration. From the inverse shape of the probability of nationalization, it is seen that in order to draw any conclusions regarding the impact of a variable its sign has to be changed. The results are very similar to those obtained using the probit test. The export concentration variable is significant and negative in both constructs (X_5 or X_{5D}), i.e. an increase raises the frequency of nationalization. The growth rate X_2 exerts a negative impact which is significant in the X_5 case but not in the X_{5D} case. The other variables have an insignificant impact at the 5 per cent level. The stock of direct investment X_1 exerts a negative impact when X_5 is used and a positive impact when X_{5D} is used. The impact of country size X_3 is positive and that of income X_4 is negative.

As in the probit test, nationalization relates predominantly to factors associated with the benefits, i.e. export commodity concentration and growth. The signs and impact of the other variables are as anticipated, with modest but not very important indirect effects of discouraging direct investment.

In Figure 6.5, the $D(\theta)$ function is given for the X_5 case. The

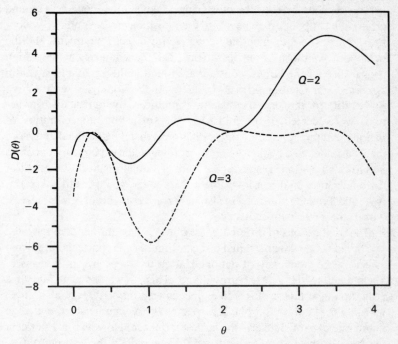

Figure 6.5 The $D(\theta)$ functions ($Q = 2$, 3) for the mixed binomial model (based on X_5)

number of mass points required for a global maximum of the likelihood function is $Q = 3$, since $D(\theta) \leqslant 0$ in this case. For $Q = 2$, $D(\theta)$ is still positive.[13] The goodness of fit measure χ^2 is high for all estimated models, owing to the poor fit of a small number of observations. The relative likelihood function based on the generalized F distribution with $Q = 1$ is very flat, which implies that there is no support in the data for choosing between probit and logit specifications.

The explanation for the different constants is related to omitted variables, or to differences in structural relationships. The calculated logistic discrimination probabilities for the highest constant (0.285 with probability 0.121 in the X_5 case) are shown in Figure 6.6. The figure can be interpreted as illustrating to what extent countries had a higher frequency of nationalization than was motivated by the explanatory variables included in the estimation. As can be seen, it is mainly countries with a high frequency of nationalization which have a high probability for the largest constant. However, it seems difficult to find any common feature of these countries which would separate them from the others.[14]

To speculate briefly, the clustering of developing countries around different mass points may be due to their position *vis-à-vis* other developing countries, with which they compete for direct investment, and the behaviour of those countries. Note that the countries with a high probability for the largest constant are found in the Middle East, Latin America and Central Africa. In fact, all the countries with a high probability for the largest constant, as predicted by logistic discrimination, were located in the midst of areas of a high concentration of nationalization. A possible interpretation is that they nationalized more than was motivated by their record according to the explanatory variables due to this position, rendering a relatively small disincentive effect of nationalization on direct investment. Moreover, countries like Algeria, Iraq, and Trinidad and Tobago also nationalized as part of 'global waves' within the petroleum industry.

The implications of different mass points can be further demonstrated by considering some marginal effects. Figure 6.7 reports the predicted effect on the frequency of nationalization produced by an increase of 1 per cent in the rate of growth X_2. This effect and that due to a reduction by a factor of 0.9 in export concentration X_5, are also given in Table 6.4, columns 1 and 2 respectively. As can be seen, a change in the rate of growth exerts the largest influence. However, a 1 per cent increase in the rate of growth would not reduce the nationalization frequency by more than 0.6 at the most. By using the most likely constant, as predicted by logistic discrimination, some of the effects become

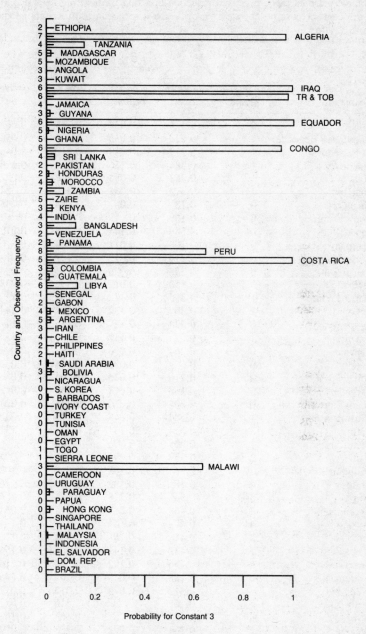

Figure 6.6 Logistic discrimination probabilities for the highest constant (based on X_5)

Table 6.4 Countrywise predicted reduction in nationalization frequency due to a 1 per cent increase in the rate of growth and a reduction in export commodity concentration by a factor of 0.9

Country	Observed frequency	1 Mean		3 Most probable mean	
		Growth rate	Concen-tration	Growth rate	Concen-tration
Brazil	0	0.3	0.072	0.288	0.06
Dominican Republic	1	0.228	0.036	0.204	0.036
El Salvador	1	0.312	0.048	0.312	0.048
Indonesia	1	0.384	0.156	0.384	0.156
Malaysia	1	0.252	0.084	0.228	0.072
Thailand	1	0.312	0.084	0.3	0.084
Singapore	0	0.18	0.06	0.156	0.048
Hong Kong	0	0.108	0	0.072	0
Papua	0	0.384	0.144	0.168	0.072
Paraguay	0	0.108	−0.012	0.084	0
Uruguay	0	0.216	−0.012	0.192	−0.012
Cameroon	0	0.288	0.096	0.264	0.084
Malawi	3	0.156	−0.012	0.492	−0.048
Sierra Leone	1	0.396	0.12	0.408	0.12
Togo	1	0.36	0.132	0.372	0.144
Egypt	0	0.324	0.12	−0.936	−1.14
Oman	1	0.3	0.132	0.288	0.12
Tunisia	0	0.264	0.096	0.24	0.096
Turkey	0	0.372	0.072	0.168	0.036
Ivory Coast	0	0.216	0.036	0.204	0.036
Barbados	0	0.168	0.012	0.132	0.012
South Korea	0	0.204	0.036	0.168	0.024
Nicaragua	1	0.384	0.048	0.396	0.048
Bolivia	3	0.324	0.132	0.324	0.132
Saudi Arabia	1	0.228	0.096	0.204	0.096
Haiti	2	0.336	0.096	0.336	0.084
Philippines	2	0.36	0.108	0.36	0.108
Chile	4	0.48	0.192	0.516	0.216
Iran	3	0.564	0.228	0.624	0.264
Argentina	5	0.468	0.084	0.516	0.084
Mexico	4	0.408	0.144	0.432	0.144
Gabon	2	0.42	0.18	0.444	0.192
Senegal	1	0.432	0.144	0.468	0.156
Libya	6	0.456	0.192	0.504	0.216
Guatemala	2	0.288	0.048	0.264	0.048
Colombia	3	0.312	0.072	0.312	0.072
Costa Rica	5	0.168	0	0.516	−0.012
Peru	8	0.492	0.18	0.468	0.168
Panama	2	0.264	0.072	0.252	0.072
Venezuela	2	0.432	0.192	0.468	0.192
Bangladesh	3	0.252	−0.06	0.24	−0.06

Country	Observed frequency	1 Mean Growth rate	2 Mean Concen-tration	3 Most probable mean Growth rate	4 Most probable mean Concen-tration
India	4	0.54	0.132	0.6	0.144
Kenya	3	0.312	0.108	0.312	0.108
Zaire	5	0.54	0.216	0.612	0.24
Zambia	7	0.528	0.228	0.588	0.252
Morocco	4	0.384	0.144	0.408	0.144
Honduras	2	0.288	0.06	0.276	0.06
Pakistan	2	0.384	0.072	0.396	0.072
Sri Lanka	4	0.384	0.096	0.396	0.096
Congo	6	0.288	0.12	0.636	0.252
Ghana	5	0.516	0.12	0.588	0.144
Nigeria	5	0.492	0.204	0.552	0.228
Equador	6	0.216	0.084	0.588	0.216
Guyana	3	0.336	0.12	0.348	0.132
Jamaica	4	0.516	0.168	0.576	0.18
Trinidad and Tobago	6	0.264	0.108	0.636	0.264
Iraq	6	0.252	0.108	0.624	0.264
Kuwait	3	0.444	0.192	0.468	0.192
Angola	3	0.564	0.168	0.552	0.168
Mozambique	5	0.552	0.12	0.612	0.132
Madagascar	5	0.468	0.108	0.516	0.108
Tanzania	4	0.312	0.072	0.312	0.072
Algeria	7	0.348	0.156	0.624	0.252
Ethiopia	2	0.444	0.084	0.48	0.084

Note: Effects are given for the predicted mean of the mixture distribution (columns 1 and 2) and for the mixture components with the highest probability as predicted by logistic discrimination (columns 3 and 4).

more pronounced (see Table 6.4, columns 3 and 4). According to these estimates, a 1 per cent increase in the growth rate for example, would reduce the nationalization frequency in Congo and in Trinidad and Tobago by 0.636, which represents several times greater effects for these countries than is predicted with the mean over the mass points. The reason is that the estimate based on the most probable mean allows complete shifts between mass points. As can be seen from a comparison of Figure 6.6 and Table 6.4, columns 3 and 4, a substantially larger reduction in nationalization is predicted with the 'most probable mean' than with the 'mean' for countries with a high probability for the largest constant, for example, Congo, Costa Rica, Ecuador, Congo and Malawi.

If the grouping around different mass points is due to the behaviour of other countries with which a country is a close substitute for direct investment, our results suggest that influences stemming from

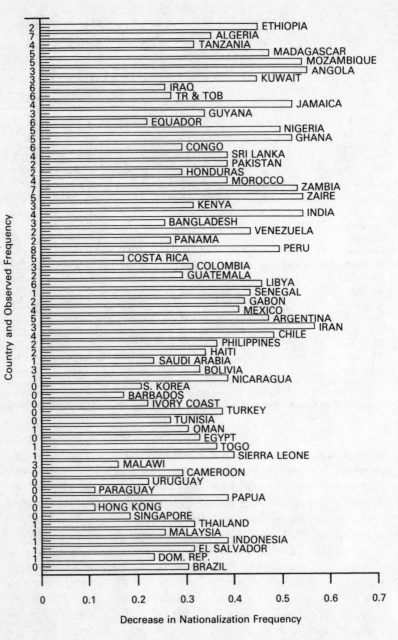

Figure 6.7 Countrywise predicted reduction in nationalization frequency due to a 1 per cent increase in the rate of growth

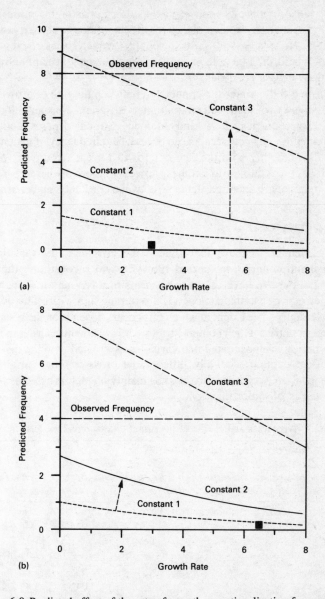

Figure 6.8 Predicted effect of the rate of growth on nationalization frequency for (a) Peru and (b) Mexico. The three effect curves give the effects on each of the three mixture components (constants 1–3) with other variables kept at observed values. The actually observed growth rate is indicated by a solid square. The arrow indicates the position and size of the switch between most likely constants as predicted by logistic discrimination.

independence between countries may explain considerably more variation in nationalization than marginal effects related to the explanatory
variables. Relatively small shifts in country characteristics or exogenous
factors would then be able to induce large changes in nationalization
behaviour across countries.

Figure 6.8 illustrates the connection between the rate of growth and
the frequency of nationalization under different constants for two
individual countries, Peru and Mexico. Similar figures could be
constructed for any country. As can be seen, the frequency of nationalization falls smoothly with the rate of growth for each constant. With a
shift from one constant to another, however, there are large potential
shifts in nationalization, particularly between constant 2 and constant 3.

CONCLUSIONS

In this chapter we have investigated the cross-country variation in
nationalization during the period 1968–79, which constitutes the peak
of the policy. We have reasoned in terms of a reputation framework,
in which acts of nationalization may discourage future direct investment
from a country. The extent to which this occurs depends on the behaviour
of other countries which compete for direct investment. During the peak
of the policy, we postulated that variables associated with the disincentive effect explain relatively little of the cross-country variation in
nationalization, which instead depends mainly on factors associated with
the benefits of nationalization.

Table 6.5 Hypotheses and results of the probit and binomial models

Variable	Expected impact related to benefits	Expected impact related to discouraging effect	Expectation of significant impact	Probit result	Binomial result
X_1		−	No	−/+ (not sig.)	−/+ (not sig.)
X_2	−		Yes	− (sig.)	− (sig./not sig.)
X_3	−	+	No	+ (sig.)	+ (not sig.)
X_4		−	No	− (not sig.)	− (not sig.)
X_5	+		Yes	+ (sig.)	+ sig.)

Note: Significance refers to the 5% level.

A study of nationalization should not focus on the number of acts or firms taken, because of the difficulties in quantifying the policy as well as the presence of reputation effects which make it crucial whether it occurs at all. Instead, we have used a probit model to explain variation in whether countries nationalized at all, and a binomial model to explain variation in nationalization frequency over time. The hypotheses set up and the results of the two model-based tests are compared in Table 6.5. The results are very similar.

Except for country size X_3 in the probit test, the results were as anticipated. The observation that economic growth X_2 and commodity concentration in exports X_5 were significant throughout, while no other variable was, suggests that cross-country variation in nationalization in the period studied can be explained by a need for foreign exchange earnings rather than by the costs of discouraging direct investment. The variables associated with the latter – the stock of investment X_1, country size X_3 and income level X_4 – generally had signs as expected but no significant influence.

Of the marginal effects, the rate of growth was found to exert the largest influence. However, the semiparametric estimator employed in the binomial model enabled unobserved heterogeneity in the data to be investigated. A clear-cut grouping of countries arose, with the constant term varying over subsets of countries. Predictions based on 'the most probable mean', which allows shifts between constant terms, magnified some of the marginal effects. The existence of subsets speaks for omitted variables or different structural relationships among groups of countries. They are in line with our notion that countries' behaviour is influenced by that of other countries with which they compete for direct investment.

In contrast with previous studies, our framework enables an explanation of the variation in nationalization over time. Our findings call for a reinterpretation of some of Jodice's (1980) results, with the political variable already excluded and the role of government unchallenged. US official development assistance matters merely because it is *one* factor influencing, in this case restricting, the extent to which a country can gain foreign exchange by nationalizing. A loss of foreign exchange in the form of US aid may directly outweigh the rents captured. Similarly, variability of export earnings matters because it is related to the need for foreign exchange, and not because it indicates policy failure. Concerning the income level, a negative impact was recorded but it was not significant. That countries with high income would have nationalized their natural resources already is an argument of little use in the case of other sectors. There is consequently no evidence that, as Jodice suggested, countries with a higher income level would nationalize more.

One way of investigating the prevalence of multiple equilibria in nationalization further would be to study the discouragement of direct investment in a period with little nationalization, and to contrast the results with those obtained here. Unfortunately, the limited cross-country variation and the dominance of mass nationalization outside the period 1968–79 prevents meaningful testing. However, the discouraging effects should also be expected to play a major role during shifts from one state to another. This matter is investigated in the following chapter.

7   Duration of nationalization

INTRODUCTION

As we have seen, the previously rising trend in the nationalization of
MNE affiliates was interrupted in the mid-1970s. Practically all countries
stopped pursuing the policy over a period of about 5 years, and there
have been very few acts in the 1980s. This seems to contradict the
mainstream theory of the obsolescing bargain (Vernon 1971), according
to which host countries' capacity to capture rents as well as run
subsidiaries on their own increases over time.

There is currently a general uncertainty regarding the reason for the
termination of the nationalization policy, and whether or not it is likely
to recur. The risk of a recurrence of nationalization is sometimes put
forward as a major cause of the low level of direct investment in developing countries in recent years. The Multilateral Investment Guarantee
Agency (MIGA), a multilateral insurance agency offering long-term
coverage (3–15 years) against non-commercial risks, was established
as a member of the World Bank Group in 1988.

In this chapter we address the question of why nationalization more
or less terminated throughout the developing world in the late 1970s.[1]
We are concerned with the broad developments, and not with phenomena
restricted to specific countries. Hypotheses are formulated and a model-
based test for the duration of nationalization is used for empirical testing.
It is considered whether there may be a risk of a return to nationalization
in the future. Indeed, it is suggested that this risk may restrain direct
investment in developing countries, despite the fact that the policy is
not pursued at present. One way of reducing this effect is to take steps
that alleviate the developing countries' acute need of foreign exchange.

The chapter is organized as follows. In the next section we discuss
previous explanations for the termination of nationalization. We then
analyse the termination of nationalization by building on the notion of

two equilibria in the market for direct investment, and generate hypotheses for empirical testing. The data, the duration model and the statistical estimation are presented next. The results of the estimation are given, and in the final section we conclude and discuss some policy implications.

PREVIOUS EXPLANATIONS FOR THE TERMINATION

Figures 6.1–6.3 illustrate nationalization of MNE affiliates during the period 1960–85. Nationalization fell from a peak in 1975 to an average of sixteen per year in 1977–9. The decline seems to have begun in the Middle East and been followed in Latin America and Africa. During this period, there was also a downturn in the number of countries which nationalized, although there was a minor revival in 1979. In the first half of the 1980s, the nationalization stabilized at a very low level. The average annual number of acts was 2.5, which is the lowest for the whole 26 year period for which data are available. The acts that did occur were mainly in Latin America and Asia. The decline was almost universal with respect to sectors; only the share of takings in agriculture increased in the period 1980–5.

No predictions had been made regarding the termination of nationalization before it actually occurred. On the contrary, on the basis of the work of Bronfenbrenner (1955) and, later, Vernon (1971) on the theory of the obsolescing bargain, it was widely expected that this policy would continue at an increasing rate. According to Vernon's theory, the developing countries improve their access to technology and export markets via the development process, which reduces the direct costs of nationalization. In addition, Gilpin (1975) prophesied deteriorating conditions for foreign investment in general owing to the decline of the US hegemony in the world economy. This can be interpreted in terms of a reduction of the indirect costs of nationalization. The termination of the nationalization policy implies, however, that the 'balance of power' has not shifted in favour of the developing countries. If it has, it is not reflected in the occurrence of nationalization.

A number of explanations for the termination of nationalization in the late 1970s, which are more or less consistent with prevailing theory, have been suggested. They can be summarized as follows (see, for example, UNCTC 1983, 1988; Kobrin 1984; Minor 1987).

1 Ventures in resource extraction are the most attractive to nationalize. By the late 1970s, all suitable targets within this category would have been taken.

2 With a decline in the terms of trade for developing countries and, in particular, a fall in commodity prices, profits would have been reduced and there would have been less rent to capture through nationalization. Like the first argument, this concerns mostly natural resource extraction.

3 MNEs would not have continued to set up vulnerable investment projects in developing countries because of the risk of nationalization. The investment flows would have declined and the developing countries would have been left without targets.

4 The developing countries would have found their experience of nationalization unsatisfactory. They would have learned that foreign investments are more valuable as a package of benefits and costs which can be manipulated.

5 The administrative, managerial and technical capabilities of host countries improved and they would have become more skilful in appropriating rents from direct investment in other ways than through nationalization.

6 Following the spurt in nationalization in the early 1970s, MNEs would have made greater efforts to make subsidiaries dependent on parent companies, increasing the direct costs of nationalization.

7 Real interest rates rose in the late 1970s, which made bank loans harder to come by. In combination with projections of dismally low commodity prices, this made the Third World willing to adjust its policies to share potential risks as well as profits with MNEs.

Some of these explanations deserve merit, but all have shortcomings as well. It can be seen from Figure 6.2, which depicts nationalization per sector, that only a modest proportion was targeted at resource extraction. Moreover, nationalization in this sector does not display a time pattern markedly different from that of other sectors. This rules out the first explanation, and casts doubt on the second, as the sole causes of the termination. However, a decline in commodity prices can affect profits not only in resource extraction itself, but also in downstream activities and, ultimately, throughout the world economy. What should really matter, however, is the level of profits that can be captured by nationalization. Changes in commodity prices constitute a subset of the factors that influence those profits. In the following, we examine the explanatory power of export prices, which ought to be related to the level of profits accessible through nationalization.

The importance of MNE defence has been much documented. Certain projects are simply not located in countries when there is a risk of nationalization. However, this is not to say that the developing countries would have been left without targets. The argument that the flows of investment would have declined prior to the termination of nationalization was refuted in Chapter 2. The major trend in direct investment to developing countries was sluggish in the 1970s, but there was no actual fall until after the peak of nationalization was over (see also Andersson and Brännäs (1990a), where the flows to individual countries are studied). There is no simple relationship between nationalizations and flows of investment.

Likewise, there is no unequivocal empirical support for the fourth explanation. As discussed by Moran (1985), the historical record provides ample examples of nationalization having turned out both as a failure and as a success story. The argument that the developing countries would have 'learned that nationalization does not pay' says nothing of why this was the case.

The fifth explanation is of a somewhat different nature. If it is correct that host countries managed to appropriate more gains through alternative measures, the termination of nationalization does not contradict the theory of the obsolescing bargain. Kobrin (1984) suggested that nationalization was more or less replaced by regulatory controls. This would have included foreign exchange and remittance restrictions, limitations on access to factor markets and on output, and changes in the rules on domestic value added, taxation and export performance requirements. It is true that there has been a sharpening of some host country policies, for example requirements for shared ownership with domestic counterparts. However, this is hardly representative of the major trend in host country behaviour.

Minor (1987) noted that the Benchmark Survey of US Investment Abroad (US Department of Commercce 1981) reported that many US subsidiaries were subject to performance requirements. What matters, however, is the development of such policies over time. Consider Tables 7.1–7.3 which summarize data for US direct investment in manufacturing in 'all developing countries', Latin America, Asia and Africa. Figures are given for 2 years: 1977 in the midst of the decline in nationalization, and 1982 when it had been completed. It is true that the data comprise only US investment, but although the policy 'level' is likely to be different for investment from different home countries (cf. Kobrin 1980), the general trends should not be. For each region, investment is tentatively divided into export oriented and import substituting (footnote to Table 7.1).

In order to provide an indication of the development of the tax base, Table 7.1 presents the net income of affiliates. As can be seen, there was generally a decline in Latin America, Africa and overall, and an

Table 7.1 Net income of manufacturing: US direct investment in developing countries, 1977 and 1982

Region	Kind of investment	Net income of affiliates ($) million) 1977	1982	Share of all developing countries (%) 1977	1982	Percentage change in share 1977–82
Total developing	Exp.	896	782	100.0	100.0	0
countries	Imp.	600	482	100.0	100.0	0
Latin America	Exp.	605	296	67.5	37.9	−43.8
	Imp.	360	30	60.0	6.2	−89.7
Asia except	Exp.	241	388	26.9	49.6	+84.4
Middle East	Imp.	232	411	38.7	85.3	+120.4
Africa	Exp.	35	18	3.9	2.3	−41.0
	Imp.	17	14	2.8	2.9	+3.6

Source: US Department of Commerce 1981, 1985
Note: Exp. export-oriented direct investment, including food and associated products, primary and fabricated metals and electric and electronic products; Imp., direct investment which substitutes for imports to the local market, including chemicals and allied products, machinery except electrical and transportation equipment. Of course, this classification is very rough. It should be noted that the period 1977–82 saw a general shift from import substitution towards export orientation within many industries.

increase in Asia. The change in the regional income shares represents first and foremost a spectacular shift from Latin America to Asia, particularly for import-substituting investment. In this category, affiliates in Latin America and Asia were responsible for 60.0 per cent and 38.7 per cent respectively of all earnings in 1977. This had been overturned to 6.2 per cent and 85.3 per cent respectively in 1982. For export-oriented investment, the corresponding shift was from 67.5 per cent and 26.9 per cent in 1977 to 37.9 per cent and 49.6 per cent in 1982.

Table 7.2 presents foreign income tax in millions of dollars, as well as the tax and income ratio. In relation to income, import-substituting investment paid on average considerably more tax than export-oriented investment.[2] For both categories, affiliates in Africa and Latin America paid the highest tax ratio, and those in Asia the lowest. Between 1977 and 1982, the Latin American and African tax ratios increased while those of Asia declined. In absolute nominal terms, tax payments increased in most cases. However, the real increase was small for import-substituting investment, and certainly negative for export-oriented investment. This is a reflection of the real decline in reported profits before tax.

Table 7.3 illustrates the development of performance requirements

Table 7.2 Foreign income taxes in manufacturing: US direct investment in developing countries, 1977 and 1982

Region	Kind of investment	Tax payments of affiliates ($) million) 1977	1982	Foreign income tax and income ratio (%) 1977	1982	Percentage change in ratio 1977–82
Total developing	Exp.	491	553	35.4	41.4	+16.9
countries	Imp.	611	884	50.5	64.7	+28.1
Latin America	Exp.	373	392	38.1	57.0	+49.6
	Imp.	431	674	54.5	95.7	+75.6
Asia except	Exp.	82	128	25.4	24.8	−2.4
Middle East	Imp.	155	180	40.0	30.5	−23.8
Africa	Exp.	24	16	40.7	47.1	+15.7
	Imp.	16	23	48.5	62.2	+28.2

Source: US Department of Commerce 1981, 1985

and investment incentives. The three regions had a fairly similar proportion of affiliates reporting subject to these policies in 1977. The proportion subject to investment incentives increased markedly in Asia and Latin America between 1977 and 1982 up to 15–16 per cent, and less so in Africa which lagged behind at about 10 per cent. However, the proportion of affiliates subject to performance requirements declined in all three regions – and more in Africa than elsewhere.

To summarize, the data show drastic changes in the inter-country distribution of profits and some differences in policy levels. but fairly uniform changes across continents in the case of the latter. Except for Asia, there was an increase in the tax and income ratio between 1977 and 1982. Nevertheless, there was only a marginal, or even negative, real increase in host country tax earnings. Meanwhile, there was a universal decline in the proportion of firms subject to performance requirements and an increase in the proportion of firms receiving investment incentives. Relatively more affluent Asia and Latin America had a more marked increase in investment incentives than Africa, while poorer Africa had the most marked decline in performance requirements.

Although there is still a multitude of host country policies that restrict the behaviour of MNEs, these changes indicate that nationalization was discontinued parallel to a stagnation in host country earnings from alternative policy measures. Meanwhile, UNCTC (1983, 1988) report increased endeavours to guarantee orderly conditions for foreign investors. Labour relations have been legislated, infrastructure provided, restrictions concerning profit repatriation diminished, special export-

Table 7.3 Investment incentives and performance requirements: US direct investment in developing countries, 1977 and 1982

Region	No. of affiliates 1977	No. of affiliates 1982	Proportion of firms receiving i.i.[a] 1977	Proportion of firms receiving i.i.[a] 1982	Percentage change in share 1977–82	Proportion of firms receiving p.r.[b] 1977	Proportion of firms receiving p.r.[b] 1982	Percentage change in 1977–82
Total developing countries	7,627	5,760	11.9	15.0	+26.0	11.0	9.0	−18.2
Latin America	4,804	3,562	12.7	16.1	+26.8	11.8	10.3	−12.7
Asia except Middle East	1,596	1,270	10.6	15.1	+42.5	8.3	6.5	−21.7
Africa	683	549	9.6	10.5	+9.4	13.7	9.7	−29.2

Source: US Department of Commerce 1981, 1985

Notes: [a] i.i., investment incentives from foreign governments, including tax concessions, tariff concessions, subsidies and other incentives

[b] p.r., performance requirements of foreign governments, including exports of a minimum amount, employment of a minimum amount of local personnel or a minimum amount of labour content in value added. Performance requirements concerning import restrictions, transfer of technology and maintenance of a specific ratio between exports and imports of inputs are not included since the statistics are less comprehensive for these kinds. However, the general trends presented in the table are unaffected by the inclusion of these other kinds of performance requirements

processing zones offering particularly generous conditions developed etc. All in all, the developing countries alleviated their burdens on direct investment and increased their endeavours to obtain new investment over the years when nationalization terminated. The fifth explanation does not account for the cessation of nationalization either.

The five explanations discussed mainly concern factors that influence the benefits of nationalization. The sixth, by contrast, is concerned with the direct costs. It argues that these would have increased owing to an improved capacity within MNEs to make subsidiaries dependent on parent companies. As a result of the rapid increase in nationalization, many MNEs switched strategy, giving up the control of, for example, extraction and processing of natural resources, while focusing on retaining control over distribution and transportation.[3] As pointed out by Milgrom and Roberts (1990), MNEs spent resources to strengthen their bargaining position. It should be recalled, however, that the theory of the obsolescing bargain prophesied falling direct costs of nationalization with the development process. This was believed to spur nationalization in the early 1970s. Why would the trend have shifted dramatically in favour of MNEs after 1975 if there was no marked decline in the flow of investment?

While the above explanations appear insufficient taken one at a time, they may together present a more convincing picture. Trying a composite explanation, we can recall from Chapter 1 that regimes in newly independent countries perceived political gains from nationalizing which contributed to setting the policy off on a large scale in the late 1960s. In particular, it was viewed as important for national pride to acquire control over a country's natural resources. Activities closely related to extraction and processing of natural resources are also among the easiest to run reasonably well under domestic ownership.

In the mid-1970s, by contrast, most developing countries were not newly independent any longer, and there were not as many attractive targets for nationalization. The home country governments had switched to a flexible strategy which offered fewer political gains from nationalization, and MNEs had adopted an effective economic defence. Thus, the political gains of nationalization had diminished along with the economic advantages. At the same time, there was an ideological change on an international scale. The support for regulatory regimes had weakened, while a greater confidence was shown in market forces. In this situation, the developing countries directed their efforts first and foremost towards learning how to gain from direct investment by co-operating with foreign investors. They dropped their plans for nationalization, as well as the most inhibiting regulations and restrictions, and instead insisted on joint ventures and developed positive investment incentives.

This scenario should reflect part of the developments that brought nationalization to an end. If it is correct, and the developing countries have actually learned how to gain from direct investment under foreign ownership, there need not be much concern about a return to nationalization in the future. However, we argue that this is not the whole story. In fact, it seems unlikely that the abrupt termination of nationalization in the late 1970s would be entirely related to a shift in any kind of benefits or direct costs. After all, it is difficult to argue convincingly that there would have been virtually no projects left for which the benefits of nationalization outweigh the direct costs. Hence, there is good reason to seek the prime cause for the cessation of nationalization within the category of indirect costs.

The strength and nature of the indirect costs to nationalization have changed over time. The threat of home country retaliation, economic or military, discouraged nationalization up to the late 1960s. Even as this factor later wore off, Jodice (1980) found that dependence on American aid exerted a negative influence on nationalization in the period 1968–76. The role of international organizations has become important. For example, in 1971 the World Bank was mandated to deny credit to countries that nationalized. Without disputing the role of home countries and international organizations, these are excluded here. As was made clear in Chapter 2, we investigate whether most country policies can be understood in terms of economic gains *vis-à-vis* direct or portfolio investment.

This is where the seventh explanation comes in. As background, consider the general deterioration of the economic environment which began in the early 1970s. After the collapse of the Bretton Woods system of fixed exchange rates, and its replacement by a regime of floating rates, huge imbalances in international payments emerged. These were accompanied by steep and abrupt changes in the terms of trade between groups of countries. Increasing and persistent inflation and unemployment followed, and there was a loss of forward momentum in world production and trade. The world economy had entered a period of growing uncertainty and instability (UNCTC 1983).

The greater uncertainty in the world economy together with a higher opportunity cost for foreign exchange caused by higher interest rates would have made it, the argument goes, more attractive for developing countries to accept direct investment and let MNEs share the risks for business operations rather than run them on their own (see Pollio and Riemenschneider 1988).[8] There are some serious question marks, however. In past studies, nationalization was generally found to be associated with balance of payments difficulties, suggesting that the objective is normally to capture short-term gains of foreign exchange when such are greatly needed. Why would balance of payments difficulties have drastically induced countries to terminate nationalization in the late 1970s?

In fact, this explanation is somewhat misleading. Real interest rates were low when the nationalization policy was brought to an end. Inflation soared in the early 1970s and made real interest rates negative through most of the decade. Moreover, commercial borrowing became available for developing countries to an extent which had never been encountered previously, enabling new attractive financing options. Real interest rates did not really climb until 1978, or even 1979. At this time, the peak of nationalization was well over.

Thus, we still do not have the whole picture. In the following, we build on the framework developed in the previous chapters, and present new hypotheses for the termination of nationalization. These are tested with the help of a duration model.

NEW HYPOTHESES

The explanations discussed above have reasoned in terms of one country–one firm interaction. As elaborated in the previous chapters, different potential host countries are, in practice, substitutes for direct investment. With a scarcity of factors that MNEs can provide, these countries can be expected to compete in order to attract direct investment, which makes it important to recognize co-ordination problems between countries. When there are two competing countries, Chapter 5 showed that a country which nationalizes alone discourages more direct investment than a country which nationalizes when its competitor does. In Chapter 6, this was extended to a framework of many countries. A notion of two global equilibria in host country behaviour was introduced, with nationalization a viable policy in either 'many' or 'few' countries. This received some empirical support as tests based on probit and binomial models verified that the cross-country variation in nationalization at the peak of the policy was related to factors associated with the benefits rather than the costs of discouraging direct investment.

To examine the notion of two equilibria further, in this chapter we analyse the termination of nationalization in the late 1970s, which is viewed as a shift from an equilibrium with nationalization to one without. The first question concerns why there was such a shift at that time. As discussed in Chapter 6, the gains made by countries that successfully attract investment from competitors who nationalize may not be sufficient to terminate this policy when it occurs in many countries. Rather, a termination should be set off by other factors, unrelated to the discouragement of direct investment. For example, there may be other indirect effects. As the number of competing countries which pursue nationalization decreases, however, those that continue would be confronted with the policy's increasingly negative impact on the undertaking of direct investment. Thus, we expect factors associated with the disincentive effect on direct investment to exert a growing impact during the termination of nationalization.

Let us review the developments in the international capital markets in the middle and late 1970s. From about 1974, the OPEC countries were unable to absorb their rapidly rising export revenues. The World Bank (1985) pointed out that they initially had a strong preference for bank deposits and favoured the Eurodollar market over domestic banking systems. The result was a swift expansion of liquidity directed towards international lending. Real interest rates fell and new borrowers were sought. Except for the macro-economic forces working to increase bank lending, there were factors specific to the behaviour of banks pushing in the same direction at the time. These were the increased efficiency of international banking, changes in the portfolio objectives and preferences of banks which made them emphasize balance sheet growth rather than the immediate rate of return, and the development of mechanisms to deal with sovereign risk through so-called cross-default clauses. Although the latter served to reduce spread and fees carried on loans and the indirect cost to nationalization, it did not make all countries eligible for lending.

In 1974 and the following years, a number of developing countries consequently found that they could borrow commercially at favourable rates for the first time. As made clear by Eaton *et al.* (1986), for example, borrowers' net worth is of little help in understanding sovereign debt. Banks estimated the prospects for default or rescheduling prior to lending, using macro-economic data as well as subjective judgements. There was a stronger incentive to secure a reputation as a reliable business partner. In other words, the improved access to commercial borrowing increased the indirect costs to nationalization.

In Chapter 6, we argued that nationalization of MNE affiliates is driven by short-term gains of foreign exchange. Our hypothesis is that some countries which previously found nationalization economically sound, when there were high rents to capture, now found that it was no longer as attractive since they could obtain foreign exchange at low cost to the extent that they abstained from nationalization. As these countries ceased to nationalize, the ones that continued found themselves more and more alone, and sensed the risk of losing future direct investment to their competitors if they continued. Thus, countries were gradually shifted to the state in which nationalization does not pay.

In order to investigate this explanation, we use a model which tests for the length of time that countries remained in the nationalization stage. Here we use the conventional term duration model (e.g. Lancaster 1979). As argued in Chapter 6, as a result of the adverse effects of nationalization on the reputation of a host country, it becomes important whether or not the policy occurs, or with what frequency in time. In any case, there are no consistent data on the size or seriousness of nationalization, the dollar value of assets taken, the amount of compensation paid etc.

Even though the countries included in the test did not nationalize every year, practically all of them displayed a more or less clear-cut sequence of acts from the rapid increase in selective nationalization in the late 1960s up to the middle or late 1970s when they ceased to nationalize. This makes it straightforward to reason in terms of the 'duration' of a nationalization stage, which is thought of as the equilibrium in which it pays to overtake direct investment selectively. The period considered is 1974–8, in which commercial borrowing was available for developing countries and interest rates were low.

Our dependent variable is *the duration of countries' nationalization stage*, measured from 1974. It takes a value of 1 for countries which nationalized for the last time in 1974, 2 for countries which did so in 1975 and so forth. The distribution of observations is shown in Figure 7.1. For model estimation, it is important to recognize that the duration variable is available in discrete (end of year months) form and is truncated at the end of 1978.

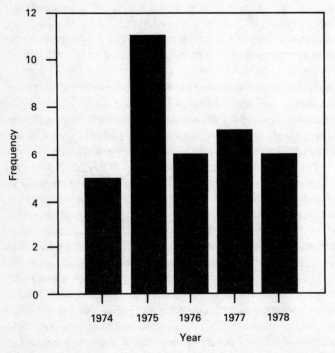

Figure 7.1 Duration of nationalization frequencies (annual data, $n = 35$)

The definitions of the explanatory variables and descriptive statistics are presented in Table 7.4. *The stock of direct investment* is the prime variable expected to be associated with the possible indirect effect of discouraging direct investment (cf. Chapter 6). The greater the stock, the more investment there is to discourage, so that there should be a negative impact on the duration of nationalization. The variable also indicates the amount of suitable targets

Table 7.4 Definitions of variables and descriptive statistics

Definition of variable		Mean	Median	Standard deviation	n
X_1	Direct investment (stock, 1974)	807	340	975	35
X_2	Average growth (1970–9)	2.6	3.6	4.7	35
X_3	GDP (1974)	12,002	2,990	20,801	34
X_4	External debt ratio (change, 1973–8)	67	33	93	33
X_5	Export price (change, 1970–8)	261	197	216	32
X_6	GDP/c (1979)	1,390	630	2,863	35

for nationalization. If that role dominates, we expect a positive impact.

The two other possible proxy variables used in Chapter 6 for the disincentive effect – GDP and GDP/c – are also included in the model test. A negative impact is expected from the latter because a higher income level implies that there is more potential direct investment to discourage. Concerning market size, the disincentive effect is expected to render a positive impact since direct investment is less easily discouraged from a larger economy. On the other hand, a negative impact may result from an increased ability to earn tax revenue from direct investment.

In Chapter 6, the *rate of growth* was found to be the major determinant of the cross-country variation in nationalization. Again, this is associated with an economy's 'soundness' or general economic performance, and should be inversely related to the benefits of nationalization. If the termination of nationalization was due to general economic improvements and a decline in the opportunity cost of foreign exchange, we can expect the rate of growth to be negatively related to the duration of nationalization. The reliance on foreign borrowing is indicated by the change in the *external debt ratio* between 1973 and 1978. A negative change has been set at zero, since only an increase would affect nationalization behaviour. Finally, given that the fall in commodity prices played a role, we expect *export prices* to exert a positive impact.

The first three explanatory variables (X_1, X_3, X_6) maintained a fairly steady level during the period of estimation, so that they are only measured in individual years. The last three (X_2, X_4, X_5) are related to the performance of countries during the sample period, which would influence the cross-country distribution of duration times. For the rate of growth, we use the average value for the whole period 1970–9, since the level over a longer time range influences the basic soundness of the economy. Likewise, changes in the export price over a longer time range are important for the level of profitability in industry. Concerning the external debt ratio, we have suggested that an increase from about 1973, when a supply of inexpensive credit emerged for the developing countries, would be negatively related to the duration of nationalization.

To summarize, the duration of nationalization is expected to be negatively correlated with foreign borrowing and positively correlated with the export price. If the indirect effects related to the risk of discouraging direct investment played an increasing role, we expect variables associated with these to cut the duration of nationalization.

DATA, DURATION MODEL AND ESTIMATION

The data base was presented in Chapter 6. The countries included here are those which undertook nationalization in the first half of the 1970s and which had, with one exception, an average stock of direct investment of at least US$60 million in 1972–4.[4] As in the previous section, countries with a smaller stock are excluded to avoid cases where nationalization ceased because practically everything had been taken. The proportions for geographic regions are as follows: South America, 0.17; Central America, 0.17; Africa, 0.46; Middle East, 0.09; Asia, 0.11.

The data are available at an annual level so that estimators designed for discretized or grouped data are appropriate. From Monte Carlo experimentation, Brännäs (1987) concluded that the most reliable estimator and test statistics for such data are, at present, based on the likelihood function. This is the approach adopted here. The specification of a density for the duration t appears less crucial with grouped data, as we have here, than for exactly observed data. In addition, we have to consider that the data are truncated to the right as the observation period is limited. The maximum likelihood estimator (ML) then maximizes the likelihood function

$$L = \prod_{i=1}^{N} \frac{F(U_i) - F(L_i)}{F(T)} \qquad (7.1)$$

where U_i is the upper limit and L_i the lower limit in months of each country's duration of nationalization. T represents the common truncation time, and N the number of observations.

In line with a number of previous studies of duration phenomena we assume that t is Weibull distributed (e.g. Lancaster 1979). The distribution function is then of the form

$$F(t) = 1 - \exp[- \Lambda(t)] \qquad (7.2)$$

where $\Lambda(t) = t^\alpha \exp(X\beta)$. The expectation of t is $\exp(-\alpha^{-1}X\beta)\,\Gamma(1 + \alpha^{-1})$, where $\Gamma(.)$ is the gamma function. Corresponding to the Weibull variable t is

$$y = \ln t = -\alpha^{-1}X\beta + \alpha^{-1}w \qquad (7.3)$$

where w is extreme value distributed. The estimates of the unknown parameters α and β in the truncated and grouped Weibull case are obtained iteratively by maximizing the logarithm of the likelihood function using a Newton-Raphson procedure. The standard errors of estimates are obtained from the Hessian matrix.

RESULTS

The estimation results are given in Table 7.5. Two runs have been undertaken: one with all explanatory variables included (the unrestricted model), and one where the three least significant variables are excluded (the restricted model). When all variables are included, none of the possible proxy variables for the disincentive effect (X_1, X_3, X_6) are significant. Except for GDP, however, the signs are as would be expected with such an effect. The rate of growth X_2, which was the major determinant of the termination of nationalization, had the smallest t value of all variables. When X_2, X_3 and X_6 are excluded, the stock of direct investment X_1 turns out to have a significant and shortening impact on the duration of nationalization. Since the stock is the most certain indicator of the disincentive effect, this should have played an important role. Moreover, an increase in the stock of investment by 1 per cent (with all other variables fixed at mean levels) shortens the duration considerably, by about 3 months according to the unrestricted model and by about 4 months according to the restricted model (cf. Table 7.5). The (statistically insignificant) effects of a 1 per cent increase in GDP (X_3) and GDP/c (X_6) are of the same order.

The disincentive effect alone does not explain the termination of nationalization. As can be seen in Table 7.5, an increase in the external debt ratio X_4 cuts the duration of nationalization, while increased export prices X_5 prolong it. Both exert a significant impact, but the marginal effects are fairly small. These variables may explain mainly

Table 7.5 Weibull model results

Variable	Estimates		Effects	
ln X_1	0.522 (1.28)	0.766 (2.91)	−2.91	−4.14
X_2	0.068 (0.58)	–	−0.79	–
ln X_3	0.325 (1.00)	–	−2.97	–
X_4	0.009 (2.23)	0.007 (2.06)	−0.07	−0.05
X_5	−0.010 (−2.50)	−0.007 (−2.63)	0.31	0.22
ln X_6	0.515 (1.11)	–	−3.58	–
Constant	−17.191 (−3.78)	−12.273 (−4.76)		
α	2.687	2.534		
H: $\alpha = 1$	(3.17)	(3.18)		
l	−35.0	−37.4		

Note: Maximum likelihood estimates (*t* values in parentheses) and estimated mean effects in months of a 1 per cent change in each mean

which countries began to terminate nationalization (X_4 and which did not do so (X_5) respectively. The disincentive effect, on the other hand, exerted a 'large impact' by explaining which countries were the least likely to discourage a great deal of direct investment and nationalized over the longest period. This gains some support from the large α estimate, which reports that the propensity to stop nationalization increased over time (positive duration dependence). In other words, the probability that a country would stop nationalizing in a certain period, given that it had not terminated previously, increased during the period studied. As more and more countries terminated, the disincentive effect increasingly prevented nationalization.

l is the value of the log likelihood function. The assumed Weibull distribution receives support from a plot of $ln[-ln(1-F^*)]$ against ln t, where the form of this particular plot is obtained from (7.2). F^* is an estimate of the distribution function. The pattern does not deviate much from a straight line, as can be seen in Figure 7.2. A plot of the expected uniform order statistic against an ordered truncated distribution function (Figure 7.3) suggests that the assumed model specification

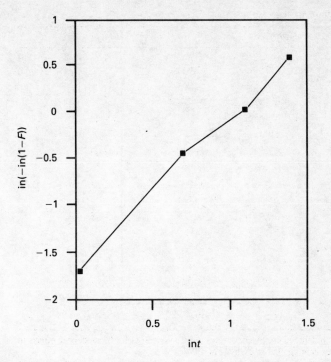

Figure 7.2 Log-log plot to test for a Weibull distribution

cannot be rejected. Again, this is due to the relatively small deviation from a straight line (cf. Cox and Hinkley 1974: Ch. 3). Attempts to use Powell's (1986) symmetrically trimmed least squares estimator for continuous but truncated data were not successful because of flatness in the criterion function.

A simple but rather weak test was performed to test whether nationalizations in each geographic region are terminated uniformly over time, or in some more clustered form. The number of times that the observed cumulative frequency exceeds the expected and hypothetical uniform cumulative frequency is approximately binomially distributed. Probabilities for the outcomes or more extreme outcomes can then be calculated. The binomial probability of three or more out of four possible ($p = 0.5$ and both cumulative frequences have equal maxima) is 0.0625. This implies that the hypothesis of a uniform termination time distribution can be rejected at the 10 per cent level. The p value for the Asian and South and Central American countries is 0.0625, for African countries is 0.3125 and for Middle East countries

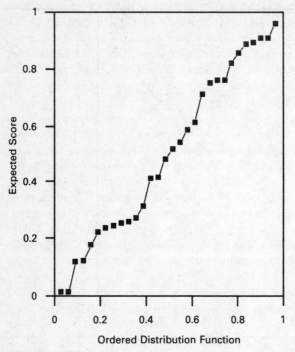

Figure 7.3 Plot of expected uniform order statistic versus ordered truncated distribution function (evaluations at mid-year months)

0.9375. Thus, there is some evidence of clustering in the Asian and American continents.

CONCLUDING REMARKS

The nationalization of MNE affiliates stopped abruptly among the developing countries in the late 1970s. The political gains of pursuing nationalization had declined as most developing countries were not newly independent any longer and the home countries had come to adopt more flexible strategies. Meanwhile, there were fewer attractive economic targets, as natural resources had often been taken already and MNEs had improved their defence against the policy. Nevertheless, these factors do not provide a comprehensive explanation for the termination of nationalization. It is unlikely that any shifts in benefits or direct costs would have left the developing countries without any targets. The prime cause of the termination must be sought within the category of indirect costs.

In this chapter we have undertaken a duration model test of nationalization in the late 1970s. An increase in the external debt ratio and a fall in export prices both exerted a significant impact on the duration of nationalization. However, the marginal effects of these variables were small. The stock of direct investment, on the other hand, was found to exert a substantial negative impact, which suggests that the costs of discouraging direct investment played a major role for the cessation of the nationalization policy. This is also supported by the positive duration dependence obtained. The two other possible proxy variables for the disincentive effect did not exert a significant impact.

The major role that the costs of discouraging direct investment played in terminating nationalization contrasts with Chapter 6, in which cross-country variation in the policy at its peak was examined. Together, these two chapters provide some tentative support for the notion of co-ordination problems and multiple equilibria in nationalization. Given that this interpretation is correct, it should be possible to verify shifts in structural relationships along with the shifts between equilibria. In order to test explicitly for this effect, it is necessary to formulate hypotheses which can be examined with the help of panel data. Again, this task is addressed by Andersson and Brännäs (1990b).

Thus, our results suggest that nationalization ceased in the late 1970s because of a combination of access to inexpensive borrowing, a fall in commodity prices and the increasingly negative impact on direct investment from continuing when most other countries had stopped. Real interest rates have been high since then and most developing countries have been constrained in their commercial borrowing. As multibillion dollar debts have accumulated and exports to the industrialized economies have been squeezed by import quotas and other kinds of protectionism, the developing countries' need of foreign exchange has become more desperate than ever. Direct investment is increasingly viewed as a favourable source of foreign capital, employment opportunities and an increase in output and exports. The observed host country policies have become more benevolent than ever, and the recent investment revival in developing countries is expected to continue over the next decade.

In the present situation, when the stock of direct investment is depressed and there are forecasts of an increase in the flows of investment, there is good reason for developing countries to abstain from nationalization. Nevertheless, if our analysis is correct, the implications for a future return to the policy may not be encouraging. If the stock of investment reaches a high level relative to the potential for continued flows, the overwhelming need for foreign exchange earnings again constitutes a motive for nationalization. Given that others would follow if one country acted, selective nationalization would start again in many countries. The obscure threat of this possibility may currently hold back direct investment from developing countries, despite the at present hospitable host country attitudes.

The endeavours of many developing countries to obtain direct investment, reduced tax rates, free profit repatriation etc. further reduce their foreign exchange earnings from direct investment, particularly because MNEs tend to repatriate excessively rather than reinvest in troubled economies. This increases the attractiveness of nationalization, the risk of which again hampers direct investment etc. The situation may not necessarily improve much with a multilateral insurance agency or louder rhetoric. It does not matter how benevolently countries promise to behave if nationalization may turn out to be profitable subsequent to the undertaking of direct investment, and MNEs do not invest in the first place if they expect that to happen, even if there is to be full compensation. The acute scarcity of foreign exchange in developing countries has to be addressed if more direct investment is to be realized.

Part IV

Conclusion and policy implications

8 Conclusions

INTRODUCTION

The findings of this book can be said to reinforce two generally accepted views. On the one hand, host country policies that manipulate the behaviour of firms do not prevent or distort the pattern of direct investment. On the other hand, policies that manipulate the ownership and control of firms may do so. Here, these states have been shown to prevail in a market where both host countries and firms compete for gains from direct investment.

While the findings so far can be said to conform with general wisdom, new insights have been provided as to the extent to which taxation and nationalization can be expected to be observed under different circumstances. In turn, this has implications for the distribution of gains from direct investment between host countries and firms. Concerning taxation, a comparison with Doyle and van Wijnbergen (1984) highlights the difference between our findings and those that have been previously reported in the literature. In their study, the irreversible cost of undertaking direct investment is shifted onto a host country by means of a tax holiday. Instead, we found that host country competition shifts the whole surplus from production (net of the irreversible cost) to a multinational firm. Concerning nationalization, it has been shown that the policy might prevail selectively over extended periods of time, which has implications for the efficiency of the capital markets.

Furthermore, the studies undertaken underline the applicability of strategic analyses to the market for direct investment, taking into consideration the interaction between countries as well as firms. Using a game-theoretical approach, it has been demonstrated that the behaviour of different countries *vis-à-vis* direct investment may be interdependent and subject to co-ordination problems. The theoretical models have generated hypotheses which have been subject to some empirical testing.

Consequently, we have provided partly new explanations of the extent to which countries nationalized foreign direct investment in the 1970s (cf. Jodice 1980) and of the termination of the policy in the late 1970s (cf. Kobrin 1984; Minor 1987).

In this final chapter we discuss, first, some implications for empirical work on direct investment and its impact on host countries and, second, the policy implications.

IMPLICATIONS FOR EMPIRICAL STUDIES

The models developed have, of course, been crude simplifications of the real world, and there are many possible qualifications and extensions. As discussed on pp. 33–4, the two kinds of host country policies considered, taxation and nationalization, are just two extreme points on a continuum of options. In practice, it is important to consider *all* the policy options that might be available for a host country, as well as the possible combinations. Likewise, it is important to note that direct investment itself is only an extreme variant of foreign business activities. There are other forms which involve less than full control by a foreign firm.

The possibility that a host country will require joint ventures is a case in point. By making a foreign firm give up some of its ownership and control to a domestic firm, the creation of a joint venture may affect both the control and the behaviour of an affiliate. Studying the circumstances under which stimulation of joint ventures dominates pure taxation or nationalization when there is competition between potential host countries is one extension of the present study which may be worth pursuing. It would also be interesting to investigate whether changing attitudes to joint ventures contributed to the discontinuation of nationalization in the late 1970s.

It may be recalled that the empirical tests of nationalization have been limited to a partial study of the frequency of nationalization in one period, and the termination of the policy during another. These tests should preferably be included in the same model. Moreover, there are two additional weaknesses. First, the endogenous variables are recorded year by year, while the exogenous variables are calculated only as average values for the period studied. Second, it would be desirable to have both nationalization and investment flow determined endogenously within the model, instead of merely using proxy variables for a country's ability to attract direct investment.

Both these limitations hinge on the availability of data. Requiring data on exogenous variables or investments year by year reduces the number of countries for which data can be obtained, and also introduces greater uncertainty concerning the quality of the data. Using a simultaneous equation model, however, Anderson and Brännäs (1990b) provide a joint explanation of nationalization and investment flow in fifty-seven countries.[1] Nevertheless, further studies are required before we can claim to have a full understanding of the pheonomenon of widespread nationalization in developing countries (possibly a unique outburst of the 1970s). Hopefully, we have been able to attract attention to the need to incorporate the interaction between host countries as well as firms in the analysis.

Returning to taxation, the approach used in this book can be applied to developed as well as developing countries, and the degree of competition between alternative host countries might not be viewed as stagnant but rather as subject to change. For example, Andersson (1990) analyses the completion of the Single European Market by 1992 and the opportunities open to individual European Community (EC) countries to tax or impose local content rules on inward direct investment. The more integrated that individual EC countries become, the closer competitors they are for direct investment targeted at the Single European Market as a whole. This has implications for the ability of the EC to pursue a protectionist policy when investment projects can be set up within it. Developing this theme, there is a need for joint analyses of the openness of goods markets and the functioning of capital markets.

A critical assumption in this study is the prevalence of a trade-off in the gains of a host country and an investing firm. This construction can hardly be refuted altogether. Tax payments represent costs to an MNE, but government revenue for a host country. Spin-off effects on the productivity of domestic firms is desirable for a host country, but may mean that competitors to the MNE arise. Pollution abatement means that negative environmental effects are forgone for a host country, but it leads to higher costs for an MNE etc. However, there are cases in which the present study must be supplemented by strategies which do not involve a direct trade-off in gains. For example, policies which inspire the introduction of more efficient technology, or greater spillovers to domestic firms, may increase the total gains to be shared by a foreign firm and a host country.

In our models we have assumed that a host country taxes an individual project as much as it can. An MNE, however, does everything it can to reduce its tax payments. In practice, we cannot separate the host country–MNE tax bargaining game from its broader economic and social context. Economic success is often best promoted through the creation of mutual trust in long-term relationships. The analysis of taxation undertaken here, which can be said to focus on the prevalence of outside opportunities in bargaining, needs to be supplemented by studies of long-term relationships between multinational firms and host countries.

Finally, it should be noted that we have assumed fully informed host countries and firms which maximize their social gains and profits from direct investment. The outcome of our studies would have changed dramatically with other assumptions on these points. In practice, there is often incomplete and asymmetric information (see, for example, Milgrom and Roberts 1987), or players may have different objectives from those assumed here.

Some studies, such as those of Jodice (1980) and Kobrin (1984), have suggested that non-economic motives play an important role in the actions of host countries *vis-à-vis* MNEs. Persson and Tabellini (1989) and Romer (1990) represent new attempts to analyse government policies when there is a disproportionate political power for asset holders. In the case of host country policies, however, there is not yet any sensible formulation of non-economic motives which would lay a basis for an empirical examination. On the part of MNEs, we have similarly noted the role of objectives other than those that can be immediately related to profit maximization. Against this background, it would be desirable to carry out empirical studies that evaluate the motives of host countries and MNEs with regard to each other. Consideration of the prevalence of asymmetries in information (for example, transfer pricing), public choice approaches to the motives of host country regimes and refined representations of MNE objectives could further clarify the functioning of the market for direct investment.

POLICY IMPLICATIONS

The developing countries generally suffer from a lack of capital, as well as from a frequent acute shortage of foreign exchange. A large number of factors contribute to this state: rudimentary financial markets, the accumulation of foreign debts when interest rates were low (that now require burdensome interest payments), barriers to trade in industrialized countries, imperfections in international capital markets that lead to credit rationing, unsound macro-economic policies in developing countries which themselves give rise to overvalued exchange rates etc. As labour is abundant and capital scarce relative to the industrialized countries, there should in many instances be a high rate of return on foreign investment.

Developing countries also tend to encounter other forms of factor scarcity which are pivotal for development: technology, human capital, entrepreneurial skills etc. Attracting foreign direct investment is increasingly viewed as a favourable means of obtaining capital as well as these other complementary factors of production. This book has taken the potential for mutual gains for a multinational firm and a host country as its point of departure. Given fully informed countries and firms that act to maximize their social and financial gains from direct investment, there is no chance that any party would lose from its undertaking. Again, we do not know under what circumstances these assumptions really apply, and therefore it cannot be argued that countries should always welcome foreign direct investment. The only possible advice in this context is for a host country regime to strive towards the maximization of its social gains, and to acquire the best possible information as a basis for its design of adequate policies. Given that a regime actually has other objectives than to favour social welfare, opposition groups should seek to disclose what these objectives really are and how they manifest themselves, rather than putting the blame for damage on MNEs.

As the discussion on the multiplicity of host country gains shows, there are ways for countries to gain from direct investment without harming the activities of MNEs. The most obvious channel is that of positive spillovers, which should not be against the interests of MNEs as long as they do not raise direct competition. There are many instances in which it is possible to stimulate such spillovers in, for example, human capital or technology for pollution abatement without causing great harm to MNEs.

Thus, as a first best choice host countries should stimulate mutual gains for themselves and MNEs. At the same time, they must be expected to act in a way that enables them to earn as much tax as possible, from direct investment without discouraging it from coming in, or from leaving. MNEs, on the other hand, act to reduce host countries' ability to tax. This suggests that countries should seek to become more remote substitutes for direct investment, while firms would want them to become more similar.

By obtaining special quotas in trade with developed country markets, for example, an individual country may lessen its substitutability as a location compared with others. On the other hand, such quotas will in many instances have the most undesirable effect of preventing a country from expanding its exports. For import-substituting investments, a country may make it more difficult to reach its market from other alternative host countries. However, if the investment opportunities of a country are superior to those of its neighbours, it should strive for liberalized trade regimes in order to attract investments that target those other markets as well as its own. Since more trade enables greater profits to be shared, and the imposition of trade restrictions can be expected to result in retaliation, a general openness which allows investments to exploit opportunities in both directions seems to be the most sensible option.

Rather than advising the individual agents in the market for direct investment, however, the findings presented here mainly lend themselves to policy implications for interference by the international community in the market for direct investment. A *raison d'être* for such interference implies that it is in the interest of both firms and countries.

It is well known that efficient capital markets should make the marginal rate of return in different countries equal to the international interest rate. It is equally accepted that imperfections in the international capital markets may prevent portfolio investment from achieving this goal and make countries subject to credit rationing. A simple stimulation of capital flows from developed to developing countries is not at all certain to remedy the situation, as exemplified by many misused loans as well as aid projects. In the event that political risk prevents a transfer of capital, however, this is highly unfortunate. Indeed, Lucas (1990: 96) concludes that 'only in so far as political risk is an important factor in limiting capital flows can we expect transfers of capital to speed the international equalization of factor prices'.

Again, this study suggests that taxation of MNE affiliates does not normally prevent or distort the undertaking of direct investment as long as there is effective competition between host countries. There would consequently be no *raison d'être* for interference with host country policies that manipulate the behaviour of subsidiaries. This is applicable to direct investment which gives rise to external economies, meaning that there is no pollution control among countries for example. Inter-country policy co-operation may still be motivated by the gains of speeding up technical progress in pollution abatement. Similarly, there may be a rationale to put pressure on individual governments to strive for a socially optimal level of environmental protection, particularly when the costs of environmental degradation hit other countries as well. The point made is that the MNE–host country relationship does not *per se* pose any need for interference by the international community with national levels of pollution control.

Host country policies which interfere with the ownership of MNEs, however, may prevent direct investment from being undertaken and possibly distort the pattern of direct investment. All agents in the market for direct investment should seek a state in which countries are not lured into nationalizing, since it will discriminate among certain investment projects in the first place and therefore stop short of maximizing the potential gains from direct investment. Competition between potential host countries for gains from direct investment does not rule out the occurrence of selective nationalization because 'many' countries may pursue them and thereby avoid losing projects to each other.

In this study we have argued that nationalization becomes increasingly probable, the greater the pressure on foreign exchange in developing countries. With direct investment prevented by the risk of a return to nationalization among host countries, the latter make increasingly large concessions in order to attract investment. This further depresses their availability of foreign exchange and increases the risk of a return to nationalization when firms actually do undertake direct investment.

The substantial decline in direct investment that has occurred in most of the Third World in the 1980s may signal that investors, in fact, do sense a risk of a return to nationalization. The World Bank (1987) and UNCTC (1988) have prophesied a rapid increase in direct investment in the late 1980s and 1990s. If our conclusions are correct, an investment revival is likely to be hampered. This is detrimental to both MNEs and the developing countries, and provides a *raison d'être* for interference in the market to rule out the risk of nationalization.

The establishment of a multilateral insurance agency (MIGA) within the World Bank in 1988 represents an effort to curb the adverse effects of a risk of, for example, nationalization. In contrast with national guarantee programmes, it is the result of common efforts on the part of capital-exporting and capital-importing countries to encourage equity investment, especially in the developing countries. In the event of expropriations, breaches of contract and wars or civil disturbances, a guarantee holder is entitled to compensation in accordance with well-specified contracts. Any disputes between guarantee holders and MIGA in connection with contracts are to be settled in accordance with arbitration rules.

It is doubtful to what extent MIGA can help to spur direct investment. Firms do not invest in the first place if they expect to be nationalized, even in the event of full compensation. In any case, they would have to pay the insurance fees. Under the present circumstances, when the stock of direct investment is depressed and the majority of the developing countries do not nationalize, there is actually little immediate threat of outright nationalization. The risk which has to be taken seriously is that of a widespread return to nationalization at a future stage when more investment projects have been established but the developing countries still suffer from a scarcity of foreign exchange.

Thwarting the economic rationale for nationalization is a matter of altering the costs and benefits associated with the policy among many developing countries. An effective strategy towards this end would both impose obligatory retaliation by the international community, which warrants palpable indirect costs for countries which nationalize, *and* relieve the fundamental causes of the developing countries' urgent need of foreign exchange. The latter must encompass an alleviation of excessive debt burdens rather than temporary solutions which only serve to pile new debt on top of old. Measures which seek one without the other run the risk of achieving no results. Hardly any promise of costly retaliation against countries that nationalize is credible in the face of many dissidents. Multinational enterprises will not respond to investment opportunities, no matter how profitable, if they do not expect to be able to capture the gains.

One component in a strategy designed to support a non-nationalization regime world-wide may be an organized 'supervision' of the indicators likely to trigger the policy, and a preparedness for preventive actions in times of distress. Those indicators could be, for example, the potential profits under domestic ownership relative to those captured by host countries under foreign ownership, the developing countries' terms of trade, the barriers to exports from these countries, the potential future flows of direct investment, the development of interest rates and rates of discounting etc.

Of course, the risk of a return to nationalization must not be used as a threat by the community of developing countries. All parts ought to become committed to a state in which direct investment is not discouraged by the fear of a return to the policy. The question of whether the distribution of gains between MNEs and host countries may be considered 'unfair' is a completely different matter. Adjustments of the distribution of gains should be undertaken by other means than allowing for nationalization of affiliates.

Notes

1 Statement of the issues

1 Another common term is transnational corporations (TNCs), which implies that firms can no longer be associated with a certain home country but are truly global in nature. The term MNE is used in this study, since it is the belief of the author that the firms in question generally do view their country of origin as 'home'. Other countries in which MNEs set up subsidiaries are throughout viewed as 'host countries'.

2 The results are largely found in Vernon (1977).

3 The convention has been signed by fifteen capital-exporting and fifty-six capital-importing countries. In principle, MIGA offers coverage of three types of non-commercial risks: transfer and convertibility restrictions, expropriations, and wars/revolutions/civil disturbances (MIGA 1988).

4 It has been said that Britain balanced the benefits of stable legal structures and the costs of eroding local authority, and therefore shunned military intervention where the local legal structure was satisfactory. The spurt in colonialism in the late nineteenth century was partly due to competition between the colonial powers, threatening the supremacy of Great Britain, (cf. Hobsbawm 1968; Platt 1968; Lipson 1985). Still, the over-representation of commercial ties with the colonial powers indicates that, in many instances, colonialism enabled the establishment of monopolies and excessive profits.

5 The Charter was adopted by a vote of 120 in favour, six opposed and ten abstentions. The negative votes were directed at the Charter's section on nationalization, and in particular the omission of any reference to an obligation of compensation (Sigmund 1980).

6 Similarly, Moran (1985: 15) concluded that MNEs do not do well in much politicized head-to-head public confrontations with host authorities.

7 Kobrin (1984) identified mass nationalization according to three criteria: at least fifteen acts over the 20 year period 1960–79, distribution of expropriations over a number of sectors and some evidence that ideological motives played a major role.

8 Most of this is not directly relevant to this study, and is therefore not discussed further here. See UNCTC (1988 340–62) for an overview.

9 Figures for the 1960s and 1970s are from UNCTC (1983: 17) and those for the 1980s are from the World Bank (1985, 1987) and UNCTC (1988: 74).

10 Whether direct investment is accepted in services is important for the future potential flow to developing countries. The share of services in US outward investment rose from 24 per cent 1975 to 34 per cent in 1985. The corresponding figures for Japanese outward direct investment were 36 per cent and 52 per cent respectively. Many developing countries still view direct investment in services with scepticism. See further Blomström and Lipsey (1988) and UNCTC (1988).

2 Theoretical background

1 Much work has continued to concentrate on how direct investment relates to, and affects, the pattern of trade. Some general equilibrium models have been constructed (e.g. Helpman 1984; Markusen 1984; Ethier 1986; Horn and Ethier 1988). This literature is still at a premature stage, however, and is crippled by the fact that the eclectic theory does not generate well-specified hypotheses. Rather than a theory, it is a taxonomy, enumerating factors but not specifying how they relate to each other.

2 In line with Lall and Streeten (1977), we think of 'licensing' as sales of technology, brand names, patents, services etc.

3 With trade within their organizations, MNEs benefit from absence of barriers to trade both as buyers and sellers. Therefore we could expect them to curtail the growth of protectionism. However, there is no convincing empirical evidence in this direction (cf. UNCTC 1985a; Bhagwati 1988).

4 The categorization is not complete nor are the categories mutually exclusive. In practice, compensation may soften the effect of nationalization, requirements of joint ventures be linked to measures which affect the behaviour of MNEs etc.

5 We do not consider takeovers which are contracted from the beginning. This has mostly been an option for a few developing countries richly endowed with natural resources.

6 An investment project unaffected by a takeover is independent of the parent company, which seems to contradict the internalization theory. However, a parent firm which was necessary when a subsidiary was set up need not be essential for continued profitability.

7 This discussion partly builds on Hines (1987), who argued that the Tax Reform Act of 1986 reinforced a negative incentive for US firms to invest in low-tax countries.

8 The tax rate in a particular host country also matters because an MNE often has a considerable ability to transfer profits between different host countries.

9 See De la Torre and Neckar (1988) for references to approaches incorporating quantitative as well as qualitative assessments.

10 Compare the flow of direct investment to the major regions of developing countries in the period 1970–80 (Table 1.1) with Figure 6.1, which depicts nationalizations across regions.

3 Taxation of multinational enterprise affiliates by competing host countries.

1 Most tax reform proposals are nowadays consistent with the theoretical arguments. For example, uniform taxes on assets have been advocated by the Carter Report (1966), the Meade Report (1978) and the Canadian MacDonald Commission Report (1985).

2 Moreover, the lack of success in empirical studies to demonstrate discouraging effects of shifts in host country policies on direct investment, applying even to outright nationalizations, was discussed in the previous chapter.

3 Contrary to what is sometimes asserted, the subgame perfect equilibrium does not rule out incredible threats altogether. See further Segerström (1988a), who discusses a number of requirements for this to be fulfilled. The qualifications are not necessary for our analysis, however, and are therefore ignored here.

4 There are no exogenous forces in the model, so that what does not pay today cannot pay tomorrow either when nothing is done. A firm which chooses not to invest will therefore never invest.

5 This is not a repeated game in the true sense since events are not exactly repeated period by period. Nevertheless, we can speak in terms of 'repetition of the game', referring to repetitive investment in the two countries.

6 It is assumed that a firm earning the same from production in a subsidiary as from the best alternative chooses production. Thus, we do not need strict inequality.

7 By analogy with the case of the firm, lexicographic preferences can be assumed to make a country prefer production at a zero tax to no production. For example, it is plausible that a country prefers a large to a small industrial sector when there is no difference in terms of income.

8 The role of S in model 2, in contrast with model 1, is to realize effective host country competition. In this section, this is already ensured by the investment incentives.

9 Analogous with Figure 3.2, the outcome can be illustrated in coalitional form. Case 1 is characterized by the positively sloping $t = 1$ line intersecting the vertical axis above the negatively sloping $t = 2$ line. The distance between their respective intersections measures what C_2 can tax *ex post* in $t = 1$.

4 Foreign exchange versus pollution

1 It is well known that there may be 'global irrationality' in the uncoordinated behaviour of individual nations with respect to common resources such as the oceans or the atmosphere (Ward and Dubos 1972; Dasgupta 1976). Likewise, there may be environmental spillovers across national boundaries through rivers, oceans or the atmosphere, for example.

2 Walter (1975: 28) identified four sources of environmental effects in the economic process: material source pollution (caused by extraction and transport of natural resources), process pollution, product pollution and residual pollution (related to the disposal of products once they have lived

out their useful lives). Production pollution can be said to encompass the first two, and consumption pollution the last two.

3 See UNCTC (1985b: 35) for background data and further references.

4 Gladwin (1977) identified firm-specific characteristics in organization and management which seem to influence the MNEs' environmental record.

5 It should be noted that the 'very poor' countries, which had the most lax environmental protection, accounted for some 70 per cent of the population of developing countries while receiving some 2.6 per cent of direct investment in 1980–82. This is only a slightly larger share than 10 years earlier.

6 The realization that development and environmental protection are not only compatible but interdependent represents a major change of view, articulated particularly in the Brundtland Report (WCED 1987).

7 There are three major conditions for a perfect capital market. First, the marginal utility of consumption each period should equal the discounted utility of wealth. Second, investment should be undertaken each period until the marginal product equals the cost of the capital. Finally, the discounted value of consumption should equal the discounted value of productive wealth.

8 Plants and animals may be unkown at the time of their extinction. For example, according to some estimates, 10,000 species are currently lost each year in the tropical rain forests. For an indication of some potential benefits forgone, it can be noted that a quarter of the prescription drugs used in the United States derive from plants from the tropical forests (*Economist* 1988).

9 One possible technique for estimating such values is to use implicit markets, in which the consumption of ordinary goods is linked to environmental values. Another alternative is to create artifical markets, which normally means asking consumers about their willingness to pay, referred to as contingent evaluation. Considerable difficulties pertain to both techniques, which may also be costly.

10 For a survey of international environmental co-operation, see UNCTC (1985: 75–84) where further references can be found.

5   Nationalization of multinational enterprise affiliates by competing host countries

1 It may be asked whether the optimal tax is influenced by the possibility to nationalize. While there may be some adjustment, it is possible to simplify by separating the determinants of the two policies. The optimal tax depends on a range of factors, among which the risk of nationalization exerts only a marginal impact. Not all projects are vulnerable to such risk, while 'all' projects are subject to the possibility of paying some tax.

2 The question arises as to whether an MNE can prevent nationalization from paying by raising π^N or raising ϕ (with a bribe, for example). Compare with Magee (1977) and Eaton and Gersovitz (1984) who analyse how the threat of nationalization may distort the choice of technology.

However, it is unclear how an MNE could bribe the host country without being nationalized anyway. Concerning π^N, an MNE can certainly reduce it in some activities, but not in all. Here, we neglect the MNEs' opportunity to raise ϕ or reduce π^N

3 There are other alternatives as well (cf. Sergerström 1988b), but these do not work in our set-up because of the limited choices available to the players.

4 It can be argued that, in practice, π^N falls with the amount of nationalization due to scarce entrepreneurial capacity in the host country, for example. Incorporating this in the model would reduce the amount of nationalization, but not overthrow the nature of the results.

5 With equality we obtain a very 'shaky' equilibrium, since the host country is indifferent between nationalizing everything and nationalizing the optimal selective amount. This kind of equilibrium should then be referred to as 'weak best reply dominated equilibrium'. We abstain from this qualification, and view the equality as representing the approximate equilibrium.

6 This could also be due to other plausible firm-specific characteristics in, for example, risk-aversion, technology, access to information, informal linkages to governments etc.

7 It can be noted that with μ larger than unity the π_B axis is not orthogonal to the π_A axis as in Figures 5.4 and 5.5, but the angle between them is less than 90°. Say that, when $\mu = 2$, it is 45°. For a given λ, the relocating effect along the diagonal line from country A to country B is twice as large as when $\mu = 1$. The two countries can then be interpreted as twice as close substitutes for direct investment. If $\mu = \infty$, the two axes are parallel and the slightest difference in the risk of nationalization makes any project locate in the country with the lower risk.

8 A country's gain (u^{Na}) is equivalent to the net gain u^N when both countries nationalize minus the discouraging effect, u^a when a country nationalizes alone *plus* the union of the discouraging effects in the two cases (represented in Figure 5.5. by the region which is both negatively and positively hatched).

9 Compare with (5.10), where the discount factor exerts a negative influence on the optimal amount of selective nationalization.

6 Cross-country variation in nationalization

1 This chapter builds on joint work with Kurt Brännäs, University of Umeå. See Andersson and Brännäs (1989).

2 'Others' include utilities, transportation, communications and trade. Natural resources include mining as well as petroleum.

3 Among the major nationalizations driven primarily by political motives we can mention those in the Soviet Union (1918), Eastern Europe (late 1940s and 1950s), Cuba (1959), Indonesia (1965) and Tanzania (1967). Concerning political ideological motives behind nationalization, see Vernon (1971) and Lipson (1985).

4 These shares differ from those given by Kobrin (1980), which are

based on 1960–76 only.

5 The importance of short-term foreign exchange earnings as a motive for nationalization is supported by observations of countries' indebtedness and servicing requirements, level and diversification of export earnings and exposure to commodity price fluctuations. Other related factors concern the trade regime, monetary and exchange rate policy, the rigidity of import requirements etc. (cf. De la Torre and Neckar 1988).

6 Among them were, for example, Iran, Nicaragua, Mexico and Bolivia.

7 Zimbabwe, Mauretania and Guinea had missing values. The remaining countries and the number of years in which they nationalized can be seen in Figures 6.6 and 6.7, and Table 6.4.

8 The countries excluded because of a small stock of investment all have low GDP or GDP/c indicating a small capacity to attract direct investment. Their exclusion is motivated by our aim of seriously testing the role of effects related to the discouragement of direct investment. The following countries nationalized but were excluded because of a small stock; Antigua, Afghanistan, Burma, Cambodia, Laos, Nepal, Benin, Chad, Central African Republic, Sierra Leone, Swaziland, Somalia, Uganda, Abu Dhabi, Bahrain, Dubai, Lebanon, Oman, Quatar, Syria and Yemen. An additional twenty-two countries with a very small stock did not   nationalize.

9 Because high growth also enhances a country's capacity to attract direct investment, it may be associated with the disincentive effect. That would then render a negative impact as well. If that is so, we expect the other proxy variables for that effect to be significant also.

10 The second and third runs generated fairly similar estimates. However, the explanatory power of the second is the highest, except for the SSR weighted.

11 This and the subsequent section are based on joint work with Kurt Brännäs, University of Umeå, see Andersson and Brännäs (1989).

12 The routine used is AMOEBA in Press *et al* (1986).

13 It is the same in the X_{5D} case.

14 It has been suggested that these countries would have a greater political stability and at the same time strong national sentiments. It is doubtful, however, whether this could be statistically verified. As mentioned, the converse allegation made by Jodice (1980), that political instability explains the propensity of countries to nationalize, has been refuted by previous studies.

7 Duration of nationalization

1 This chapter is based on joint work with Kurt Brännäs, University of Umeå (See Andersson and Brännäs 1990a).

2 This is in line with the competitive conditions discussed in Chapter 2. For export-oriented investment, there is primarily competition between host countries; for import-substituting investment, competition is primarily between firms. This suggests a higher tax and income ratio for the latter kind.

3 See Lipson (1985) or Moran (1985) for different strategies.
4 The exception is Libya, which is unique in that it lost half its stock of direct investment in the last year that it nationalized (1974). This dramatic reduction suggests that Libya nationalized to the extent that further possible targets were lost.

8 Conclusions

1 This paper is at present only available in mimeo form, but the preliminary results indicate that most of the findings of this book are borne out, and that the present framework does indeed enable us to capture a negative impact of nationalization on the flow of direct investment.

References

Aliber, R.Z. (1970) 'A theory of direct foreign investment', in C.P. Kindleberger (ed.) *The International Corporation: A Symposium*, Cambridge, MA, MIT Press.

Amemiya, T. (1981) 'Qualitative response models: a survey', *Journal of Economic Literature* XIX, December, 1483–536.

Andersson, T. (1990) 'Antidumping, direct investment and local content rules in the EC 1992', Research Paper 6400, Stockholm School of Economics.

Andersson T. and Brännäs, K. (1989) 'Economic factors affecting the nationalization frequency', Paper presented at the European Meeting of the Econometric Society, Munich.

Andersson, T. and Brännäs K. (1990a) Duration of nationalization', mimeo, Stockholm School of Economics and University of Umeå

Andersson , T. and Brännäs, K. (1990b) 'Explaining cross-country variation in nationalizations and investment flows over time', mimeo, Stockholm School of Economics and University of Umeå.

Areskoug, K. (1973) 'Foreign capital utilization and economic policies in developing countries', *Review of Economics and Statistics*, May.

Arrow, K.J. and Lind, R-C. (1970) 'Uncertainty and the evaluation of public investments decisions', *American Economic Review* 60, 364–78.

Barro, R. and Gordon, D. (1986) 'Rules, discretion and reputation', *Journal of Monetary Economics* 12, 101–21.

Batra, R.N. (1986) 'A general equilibrium model of multinational corporations in developing economies', *Oxford Economic Papers* 38, 342–53.

Bergsten, C.F., Horst, T. and Moran, T.H. (1978) *American Multinationals and American Interests*, Washington, DC, Brookings Institute.

Berndt, E.K., Hall, B., Hall, R.E. and Hausmann, J.A. (1974) 'Estimation and inference in non-linear structural models', *Annals of Economic and Social Measurement* 3, 653–65.

Bhagwati, J.N. (1978) *Foreign Trade Regimes and Economic Development: Anatomy and Consequences of Exchange Control Regimes*, New York, Ballinger.

Bhagwati, J.N. (1988) *Protectionism*, Cambridge, MA: MIT Press.

Binmore, K. and Herrero, M. (1984) 'Frictionless non Walrasian markets', ICERD Discussion Paper, London School of Economics.

Blomström, M. (1983) 'Foreign investment, technical efficiency and structural change, evidence from the Mexican manufacturing industry', Ph.D. Dissertation, Göteborgs Universitet.

Blomström, M. and Lipsey, R.E. (1988) US multinationals in Latin American service industries, *World Development* 17, 176–76.

Blomström M. and Wang, J. (1989) 'Foreign investment and technology transfer, a simple model', Research Paper 6363, Stockholm School of Economics.

Bojö, J., Mäler, K-G. and Unemo, L. (1990) *Environment and Development: An Economic Approach*, Dordrecht, Kluwer.

Bond, E.W. and Samuelson, L. (1986) 'Tax holidays as signals', *American Economic Review* 76, 820–26.

Brännäs, K. (1987) 'Linear regression with grouped data on the dependent variable', *Metron* XLV, 63–79.

Brännäs, K. and Rosenqvist, G. (1988) 'Semiparametric estimation of heterogeneous count data models', Paper presented at ORSA/TIMS 1988 Marketing Science Conference, Seattle.

Bronfenbrenner (1955) 'The appeal of confiscation in economic development', *Economic Development and Cultural Change* 3, 201–18.

Buckley, P.J. and Casson, M. (1976) *The Future of the Multinational Enterprise*, London, Macmillan.

Buckley, P.J. and Casson, M. (1985) *The Economic Theory of the Multinational Enterprise*, London, Macmillan.

Bulow, J. and Rogoff, K. (1989a) 'A constant recontracting model of sovereign debt', *Journal of Political Economy* 97, 155–78.

Bulow, J. and Rogoff, K. (1989b) 'Sovereign debt: is to forgive to forget' *American Economic Review* 79, 43–50.

Burton, F.N. and Inoue, H. (1984) 'Expropriation of foreign-owned firms in developing countries: a cross-national analysis', *Journal of World Trade Law* September–October, 396–414.

Caves, R.E. (1971) 'International Corporations: the industrial economics of foreign investment, *Economica* 38, 1–27.

Caves, R.E. (1982) *Multinational Enterprise and Economic Analysis*, Cambridge, Cambridge University Press.

Coase, R.H. (1937) 'The nature of the firm', *Economica* 4, 386–405.

Contractor, F.J. (1990) 'Do government policies towards foreign investment matter? An empirical investigation of the link between national policies and FDI flows', mimeo, Graduate School of Management, Rutgers University.

Cooper, R. and John, A. (1988) 'Coordinating Coordination failures in Keynesian models', *Quarterly Journal of Economics* CIII, 441–63.

Correa, C., Zalduendo, S. and Cherol, R. (1984) *Regulacion de la inversion extranjera en America Latina y el Caribe*, Buenos Aires, BID/INTAD.

Cox, D.R. and Hinkley, D.V. (1974) *Theoretical Statistics*, London, Chapman and Hall.

Dasgupta, B. (1976) *Environment and Development*, Nairobi, UNDP.

De la Torre, J. and Neckar, D.H. (1988) 'Forecasting political risks for international operations', *International Journal of Forecasting* 4, 221–41.

Diamond, P. and Mirrlees, J. (1971) 'Optimal taxation and public production', *American Economic Review* 61, 8–27, 261–78.

Doyle, C. and van Wijnbergen, S. (1984) 'Taxation of foreign multinationals: a sequentional bargaining approach to tax holidays', mimeo, Institute of

International Economic Studies, University of Stockholm.

Duerksen, C. (1983) *Environmental Regulations and Plant Siting,* Washington DC, The Conservation Foundation.

Dunn, R., Reader, S. and Wrigley, N. (1987) 'A nonparametric approach to the incorporation of heterogeneity into repeated polytomous choice models of urban shopping behaviour', *Transportation Research* 21, 327–43.

Dunning, J.H. (1977) 'Trade, location of economic activity and the MNE: a search for an eclectic approach', in B. Ohlin, P.O. Hesselborn and P.M. Wijkman (eds) *The International Allocation of Economic Activity: Proceedings of a Nobel Symposium Held at Stockholm,* London, Macmillan, pp. 395–418.

Dunning, J.H. (1981) 'Explaining the international direct investment position of countries: toward a dynamic or developmental approach,' *Weltwirtschaftliches Archiv* 117, 30–64.

Dunning, J.H. and Pearce, R.D. (1981) *The World's Largest Industrial Enterprises,* Farnborough, Gower.

Eaton, J. and Gersowitz, M (1981) 'Debt with potential repudiation: theoretical and empirical analysis,' *Review of Economic Studies* 48, 289–309.

Eaton, J. and Gersovitz, M. (1983) 'Country Risk: Economic Analysis', in R.J. Herring (ed.) *Managing International Risk,* Cambridge, Cambridge University Press.

Eaton, J. and Gersovitz, M. (1984) 'A theory of expropriation and deviations from perfect capital mobility', *Economic Journal* 94, 16–40.

Eaton, J., Gersovitz, M. and Stiglitz, J.E. (1986) 'The pure theory of country risk', *European Economic Review* 30, 481–513.

Economist (1988) 'The vanishing jungle', 15–21 October, 25–8.

Edwards, S. (1984) 'LDC foreign borrowing and default risk: an empirical investigation (1976–1980)', *American Economic Review* 74, 726–34.

Ethier, W.J. (1986) 'The multinational firm', *Quarterly Journal of Economics* November, 805–33.

Fisher, A.C. (1981) *Resource and Environmental Economics,* Cambridge, Cambridge University Press.

Freeman, M. (1979) *The Benefits of Environmental Improvement,* Resources for the Future, Baltimore, MD and London, John Hopkins University Press.

Friedman, J.W. (1986) *Game Theory with Applications to Economics,* New York and Oxford, Oxford University Press.

Fry, M. (1984) *Domestic Resource Mobilization Through Financial Development,* Vol. II *Appendixes,* Manila, ADB, Economics Office.

Gilpin, R. (1975) *U.S. Power and the Multinational Corporation,* Greenwich, New York, Basic Books.

Gladwin, T.N. (1977) *Environment, Planning and the Multinational Corporation,* Greenwich, CT, JAI Press.

Gladwin, T.N. and Welles, J.G. (1976) 'Environmental policy of multinational corporate strategy', in I. Walter (ed.) *Studies in International Environmental Economics,* New York, Wiley.

Green, R. (1972) *Political Instability as a Determinant of U.S. Foreign Investment,* Austin, TX, University of Texas Press.

Grubel, H.G. (1968) 'International diversified portfolios: welfare gains and capital flows, *American Economic Review* 58, 1299–314.

Guisinger, S. (1985) *Investment Incentives and Performance Requirements,* New

York, Praeger.

Gupta, K.L. and Islam, M.A. (1983) *Foreign Capital, Savings and Growth*, Boston, MA. Reidel.

Hajivassiliou, V.A. (1986) 'Misspecification tests for the simple switching regressions disequilibrium model', *Economic Letters* 22, 343–8.

Hajivassiliou, V.A. (1987) 'The external debt repayments problems of LDC's, *Journal of Econometrics* 36, 205–30.

Hartman, D.G. (1985) 'Tax policy and foreign direct investment', *Journal of Public Economics* 26, 107–21.

Heckman, J. and Singer, B. (1984) 'A method for minimizing the impact of distributional assumptions in econometric models for duration data', *Econometrica* 52, 271–320.

Helpman, E. (1984) 'A simple theory of international trade with multinational corporations', *Journal of Political Economy* 92, 451–71.

Hines, J.R. (1987) 'Taxation and U.S. multinational investment', mimeo, Princeton University and NBER.

Hobsbawm, E.J. (1968) *Industry and Empire*, New York, Pantheon Books.

Hood, N. and Young, S. (1979) *The Economics of Multinational Enterprise*, London and New York, Longman.

Horn, H. and Ethier, W.J. (1988) 'Managerial control of international firms and patterns of direct investment', Seminar Paper 405, Institute for International Economic Studies, University of Stockholm.

Huizinga, H. (1988) 'Country size and international tax rates', mimeo, Harvard University.

Hymer, S.H. (1960) 'The international operations of national firms: a study of direct foreign investment', Ph.D. dissertation, Massachusetts Institute of Technology.

Ishizumi, K. (1984) International commercial arbitration and federal securities regulation: reconciling two conflicting policies', *Journal of Comparative Business and Capital Market Law* 6, 81–113.

James, J. (1981) 'Growth, technology and the environment in less developed countries: a survey', in P. Streeten and R. Jolly (ed.) *Recent Issues in World Development*, New York, Pergamon.

Jodice, D.A. (1980) 'Sources of change in Third World regimes for FDI 1968–1976', *International Organization* 34, 177–206.

Johansen, L. (1982) 'On the status of the Nash type of noncooperative equilibrium in economic theory', *Scandinavian Journal of Economics* 84, 337–421.

Johnson, H.G. (1967) 'The possibility of income losses from increased efficiency or factor accumulation in the presence of tariffs', *Economic Journal* 77, 151–4.

Juhl, P. (1985) 'Economically rational design of developing countries' expropriation policies towards foreign investment', *Management International Review* 25, 45–52.

Keohane, R.O. and Nye, J.S. (1977) *Power and Interdependence: World Politics in Transition*, Boston, MA, Little, Brown.

Kindleberger, C.P. (1965) *Economic Development*, 2nd edn. New York, McGraw-Hill.

Kindleberger, C.P. (1969) *American Business Abroad: Six Lectures on Direct Investment*, New Haven, CT, Yale University Press.

Knickerbocker, F.T. (1973) *Oligopolistic Reaction and Multinational Enterprise*, Cambridge, MA, Harvard University Press.

Knudsen, H. (1974) 'Explaining the national propensity of expropriation: an ecological approach', *Journal of International Business Studies*, Spring, 51–71.

Kobrin, S.J. (1980) 'Foreign enterprises and forced divestments in the LDCs', *International Organization* 34, 65–88.

Kobrin, S.J. (1982) *Managing Political Risk Assessment: Strategic Response to Environmental Change*, Los Angeles, CA, University of California Press.

Kobrin, S.J. (1984) 'Expropriation as an attempt to control foreign firms in LDCs: trends from 1960 to 1979', *International Studies Quarterly* 28, 329–48.

Kobrin, S.J. (1986) Personal communication.

Kojima, K. (1973) 'A macroeconomic approach to foreign direct investment', *Hitotsubashi Journal of Economics* 14, 1–21.

Kojima, K. and Ozawa, T. (1984) Micro and macro-economic models of direct foreign investment: toward a synthesis,' *Hitotsubashi Journal of Economics* 25, 1–20.

Kreps, D.M. and Wilson, R. (1982) 'Reputation and imperfect equilibrium', *Journal of Economic Theory* 27, 253–79.

Kydland, F.E. and Prescott, E.C. (1977) 'Dynamic inconsistency: rules rather than discretion: the inconsistency of optimal plans', *Journal of Political Economy* 85, 513–48.

Lall, R. (1986) 'Third World multinationals', *Journal of Development Economics* 20, 381–97.

Lall, S. (1979) 'Multinational and market structure in an open developing economy: the case of Malaysia', *Weltwirtschaftliches Archiv* 115, 325–50.

Lall, S. and Streeten, P. (1977) *Foreign Investment, Transnationals and Developing Countries*, London, Macmillan.

Lancaster, T. (1979) 'Econometric methods for the duration of unemployment', *Econometrica* 47, 939–57.

Lee, J., Rana, P.B. and Iwasaki, Y. (1986) 'Effects of foreign capital inflows of developing countries of Asia', Asian Development Bank Staff Paper, 30, Manila.

Leonard, H.J. (1980) 'Multinational corporations and politics in developing countries', *World Politics* 32, 454–83.

Leonard, H.J. (1984) *Are Environmental Regulations Driving United States Industry Overseas? An Issue Report*, Washington, DC, The Conservation Foundation.

Leonard, H.J. (1988) *Pollution and the Struggle for the World Product*, Cambridge, Cambridge University Press.

Lindsay, B.G. (1983a) 'The geometry of mixture likelihoods', *Annals of Statistics* 11, 86–94.

Lindsay, B.G. (1983b) 'The geometry of mixture likelihoods, part II: The exponential family', *Annals of Statistics* 11, 783–92.

Lipson, C. (1985) *Standing Guard: Protecting Foreign Capital in the 19th and 20th Centuries*, Berkeley, CA, University of California Press.

Lucas, R. (1976) 'Ecomometric policy evaluations: a critique, in K. Brunner and A.H. Meltzer (eds) *The Philips Curve and Labor Markets*, Carnegie-Rochester Conference Series on Public Policy 1, Amsterdam, North-Holland, 19–46.

Lucas, R.E. (1990) 'Why doesn't capital flow from rich to poor countries?', *American Economic Review* Papers and Proceedings, 80 (2), 92–96.

Magee, S.P. (1977) 'Information and multinational corporations: an appropriability theory of direct foreign investment', in J.N. Bhagwati (ed.) *The New International Economic Order: The North–South Debate*, Cambridge, MA, MIT Press.

Markusen, J.P. (1984) 'Multinationals, multi-plant economies, and the gains from trade', *Journal of International Economics* 16, 205–26.

McCloskey, D.N. (1971) *Essays on a Mature Economy: Britain after 1940*, London, Methuen.

McFadden, D., Eckhaus, R., Feder, G., Hajivassiliou, V. and O'Connell, S. (1985) 'Is there life after debt? An econometric analysis of creditworthiness of developing countries' in A. Smith and J.T. Cuddington (eds) *International Debt of the Developing Countries*, Washington, DC, World Bank, 179–209.

Milgrom, P.R. and Roberts, J. (1987) 'Informational asymmetries, strategic behaviour and industrial organization', *American Economic Review (Papers and Proceedings)* 77, 184–93.

Milgrom, P. and Roberts, J. (1990) 'Bargaining and influence costs and the organization of economic activity', in J. Alt and K. Shepsle (eds) *Positive Perspectives on Political Economy*, Cambridge, Cambridge University Press.

Minor, M. (1987) 'LDCs, MNCs and changing trends in patterns of expropriation', mimeo, University of Tulsa.

Minor, M. (1988) 'Political stability and expropriation propensity: a re-examination', Paper presented at the Annual Meeting of the Southwest Political Science Association, Houston, TX.

Moran, T.H. (1974) *Multinational Corporations and the Politics of Dependence: Copper in Chile*, Princeton, NJ, Princeton University Press.

Moran, T.H. (1985) *Multinational Corporations, the Political Economy of Foreign Direct Investment*, Toronto, Lexington Books.

Multilateral Investment Guarantee Agency (MIGA) (1988) MIGA's Investment Guarantee Program, Washington, DC.

Newlon, T.S. (1987) 'Tax policy and the multinational firm's financial policy and investment decisions', Ph.D. Dissertation, Princeton University.

Papanek, G.F. (1972) 'The effect of aid and other resource transfers on savings and growth in less developed countries', *Economic Journal* 82 934–50.

Pearson, C. (1976) 'Implications for the trade and investment of developing countries of United States environmental controls', Paper presented at United Nations Conference on Trade and Development, Geneva.

Pearson, C. and Pryor, A. (1978) *Environment North and South: An Economic Interpretation*, New York, Wiley-Interscience.

Penrose, E.T. (1959) 'Profit sharing between producing countries and oil companies in the middle east', *Economic Journal* 274, 238–54.

Perrson, T. and Tabellini, G (1989) 'Representative democracy and capital taxation', mimeo, Institute of International Economic Studies, Stockholm.

Platt, D.C.M. (1968) *Finance, Trade, and Politics in British Foreign Policy, 1815–1914*, Oxford, Clarendon Press.

Pollio, G. and Riemenschneider, C.H. (1988) 'The coming Third World investment revival', *Harvard Business Review*, March–April, 114–24.

Powell, J.L. (1986) 'Symmetrically trimmed least squares estimation for Tobit models', *Econometrica* 54, 1435–60.

Prentice, R.L. (1975) 'Discrimination among some parametric models', *Biometrika* 62, 607–14.

Press, W.H., Flannery, B.P., Teukolsky, S.A. and Vetterling, W.T. (1986) *Numerical Recipes*, Cambridge, Cambridge University Press.

Robinson, R.D. (ed.) (1987) *Direct Foreign Investment, Costs and Benefits*, New York, Praeger.

Romer, P.M. (1990) 'Trade, politics, and growth in a small, less developed economy'. Paper presented at the CEPR/IIES Conference, Stockholm.

Rubenstein, A. (1982) 'Perfect equilibrium in a bargaining model', *Econometrica* 50, 97–109.

Sachs, J. (1984) 'Theoretical issues in international borrowing', Princeton Studies in International Finance 54, Princeton, NJ, Princeton University Press.

Sachs, J. and Cohen, D. (1982) 'LDC borrowing with default risk', NBER Working Paper Series 925, Cambridge, MA.

Segerström, P. (1988a) 'Renegotiation and the credibility of threats', mimeo, Stockholm School of Economics and Michigan State University.

Segerström, P. (1988b) 'Demons and repentance', *Journal of Economic Theory* 45, 32–52.

Selten, R. (1975) 'Re-examiniation of the perfectedness concept for equilibrium points in extensive games', *International Journal of Game Theory* 4, 25–55.

Shafer, M. (1985) 'Capturing the mineral multinationals: advantage or disadvantage?' in T.H. Moran, (ed.) *Multinational Corporations*, Toronto, Lexington Books.

Shaked, A. and Sutton, J. (1984) 'Involuntary unemployment as a perfect equilibrium in a bargaining model', *Econometrica* 52, 1351–68.

Shenfeld, A.B. (1984) 'Political risk and durable goods markets: essays in applied dynamic game theory', Ph.D. Dissertation, Harvard University.

Sigmund, P.E. (1980) *Multinationals in Latin America, the Politics of Nationalization*, Madison, WI, University of Wisconsin Press.

Simar, L. (1976) 'Maximum likelihood estimation of a compound Poisson process', Annals of Statistics 4, 1200–9.

Sölvell, Ö. (1987) 'Entry barriers and foreign penetration, emerging patterns of international competition in two electrical engineering industries', Ph.D. Dissertation, Stockholm School of Economics.

Svedberg, P. (1981) 'Colonial enforcement of foreign direct investment', *Manchester School of Economic and Social Studies* 48, 21–38.

Thunell, L.H. (1977) *Political risks in international business: investment behaviour of multinational corporations*, New York, Praeger.

Tirole, J. (1986) 'Procurement and renegotiation', *Journal of Political Economy* 94, 235–59.

Tirole, J. (1989) *The Theory of Industrial Organization*, Cambridge, MA, MIT Press.

Truitt, J.F. (1974) *Expropriation of Private Foreign Investment*, Bloomington, IN, Graduate School of Business, University of Indiana.

UNCTC (United Nations Centre on Transnational Corporations) (1983) *Transnational Corporations in World Development, Third Survey*, New York.

UNCTC (1985a) *Transnational Corporations and International Trade: Selected Issues*, New York.

UNCTC (1985b) *Environmental Aspects of the Activities of Transnational Corporations: A Survey*, New York.

UNCTC (1988) *Transnational Corporations in World Development, Trends and Prospects*, New York.

US Department of Commerce (1981) *U.S. Direct Investment Abroad: 1977 Benchmark Survey Data*, Bureau of Economic Analysis, International Investment Division, April.

US Department of Commerce (1985) *US Direct Investment Abroad: 1982 Benchmark Survey Data*, Bureau of Economic Analysis, December.

Vernon, R. (1966) 'International investment and international trade in the product cycle', *Quarterly Journal of Economics*, 190–207.

Vernon, R. (1971) *Sovereignty at Bay*, New York, Basic Books.

Vernon, R. (1977) *Storm Over the Multinationals: The Real Issues*, Cambridge, MA, Harvard University Press.

Vernon, R. (1983) 'Organizational and institutional responses to international risk', in R.J. Herring (ed.) *Managing International Risk*, Cambridge, Cambridge University Press.

Walter, I. (1972) 'Environmental control and patterns of international trade and investment: an emerging policy issue', *Banca Nazionale Del Lavoro Quarterly Review* 100, 82–106.

Walter, I. (1975) *International Economics of Pollution*, London, Macmillan.

Ward. B. and Dubos, R. (1972) *Only One Earth*, Harmondsworth, Penguin.

WCED (World Commission for Environment and Development) (1987) *Our Common Future*, Oxford and New York, Oxford University Press.

Weisbroad, B. (1964) 'Collective-consumption services of individual-consumption goods', *Quarterly Journal of Economics* LXXVIII, 471–7.

Williams, M.L. (1975) 'The extent and significance of the nationalization of foreign-owned assets in developing countries 1956–72, *Oxford Economic Papers* 27, 260–73.

Williamson, O. (1975) *Markets and Hierarchies: Analysis and Antitrust Implications*, New York, Free Press.

Williamson, O. (1986) *Economic Institutions of Capitalism*, New York, Free Press.

World Bank (1985) *World Development Report*, Washington, DC.

World Bank (1987) *World Development Report*, Washington, DC.

Index